DATE DUE

NO 14 '97		

Older & Growing

Older & Growing

Your Eternal Life Beginning Now

Leslie E. Moser, Ph.D.

Multi-Media Productions, Inc.

R

Multi-Media Productions, Inc.
P.O. Box 7428
Waco, Texas 76714

Library of Congress Catalog Card Number: 90-091912

ISBN 1-878-938-01-0

To Ruth, whose joy in the Lord has grown constantly and consistently before my very eyes for fifty-six years. It promises to continue to grow.

"Older and Growing"—

What a book! Here is a windfall of wisdom for all who are in the so-called "aging process." The writer exhausts every aspect of life facing those from middle life upward.

In "Older and Growing," Dr. Leslie Moser deftly deals with problems of advancing age on mental, physical and spiritual bases.

This gem of a book is desperately needed in our society. One cannot digest this marvelous message of hope without looking forward to being "older and growing" with enthusiasm and anticipation. Thank you, Dr. Moser.

Sincerely,

Dale Evans Rogers

Dale Evans Rogers

OLDER AND GROWING

Preface

I have been given the task of writing to older Christians so that their joys in the Lord may be full. That is quite a task. Many forces are at work denying full joy to older Christians.

Hopefully, I am addressing brothers and sisters who are having some experiences in common, who are feeling oppressed because of their increasing ages, and who need inspiration to make their joys full. I believe that Christians who are 50-plus would comprise a definable audience. However, we are so different one from the other that I have trouble designating any age group. But let us say this book is about Christians who are 50-plus and who are feeling stress because they are growing older. Let us hope that they can grow older while feeling that, although they are growing older, they are still growing.

Who are the Aging?

About fifteen percent of Americans are 50-plus. But in another ten years or so, that percentage is going to rise to about twenty-five percent, one-fourth of our entire population. Why is this true?

The baby boomers (persons born shortly after World Was II) have already turned forty and this group is vast. Most of them will be 50-plus in less than ten years. I can't help thinking that they are really the ones who should be reading this book. I hope they will. But, it is not too late for any of us to profit from the insights and the new information coming from the latest research studies. The baby boomers can learn to avoid some of the harsh things that are happening to 50-plus Christians right now, and they can become determined to go into the last half of their lives with optimism rather than despair.

Many Have Already Given Up

I realize that many older Christians will resist some of what I have to say. You see, the insidious and satanic forces of ageism already have the hooks in some of us. Some of us are undergoing depression and despair which, along with failing health and various catastrophic events both global and personal, are making many of us very confused and often very depressed. Some of the events you are enduring could have been avoided; some could not. But every one of us will benefit by having better attitudes about ourselves and knowing better ways of dealing with our problems.

It may be difficult for many of you to understand my optimism. Or even if you understand and agree that we should all look on the bright side, you may find you just can't do it. Some of you, without thinking much about it, have turned your disappointments and disillusionments into sharp spears of despair. Having heard how terrible old age is, you have sold out to the prophets of doom, have sold yourselves old, and have become your own worst enemies.

The goal I have in mind is to help you overcome the obstacles that you face and to lay uncompromising claim to the abundant life Christ has promised to all those who believe—not just to the young. Life should become even more abundant as we come ever and ever closer to the day when we shall see Jesus in all His beauty.

Go Along With God's Plan

It is hard sometimes to keep your joy in the Lord full with all the problems you face. I want to help you accept God's challenge and use your God-given courage, zeal, and determination to break down the gloomy prediction of a misguided society of doomsayers. They actually seem to want our golden years to be gloomy years. Many of us will rise to the occasion and make our joys in the Lord full in spite of all the forces that seem to be trying to smother us into despair. We will not give up the holy ground which is ours because we are brothers with and in Christ. He does not wish us to despair, not even for a moment. "Let not your heart be troubled...." This is His wish, and it must be our command.

OLDER AND GROWING—YOUR EVERLASTING LIFE BEGINNING NOW

TABLE OF CONTENTS:

Ch. 1   God's Greatest Gift: Life Now and Forevermore 15

Ch. 2   The Terrible Tragedy of Living Old and Dying Young.....25

Ch. 3   Aging, Defeats and Victories—Spiritual Realities..............37

Ch. 4   The Blessings of Old Age 43

Ch. 5   Chronological Age Is Secondary—Attitudes Are Primary..49

Ch. 6   Living with Vitality 63

Ch. 7   Holding On, Letting Go, and Reaching Forward...............73

Ch. 8   Living Productively with High Self-Esteem.......................81

Ch. 9   Your Sexuality—To Have and To Keep 89

Ch. 10 Social Living Through Fellowship.................................. 105

Ch. 11 Keeping Your Mind Sharp...113

Ch. 12 How Is Your Memory? 125

Ch. 13 Love of Family and Aging... 135

Ch. 14 Retirement—Should You Ever? 149

Chapter 1

GOD'S GREATEST GIFT: LIFE NOW AND FOREVERMORE

I have fought a good fight, I have finished my course, I have kept the faith. (II Timothy 4:7)

A few weeks ago I attended the morning worship service with a neighboring congregation. A large part of the song service was performed by the young people of the church. The young folk moved to the platform; and, with guitars and piano accompaniments, they sang a number of enlivening choruses for the congregation. With some choruses the congregation was asked to sing along. The words were projected onto a screen so that everyone could join in.

Hope and Reality

My heart was especially touched by one of the choruses the young people sang. It was a catchy little tune familiar to most of you, I'm sure. The name of it was "Say I Do."

The words to that song go something like this: "Anybody here want to live forever? Say I do!" This song obviously was used often in the church and had become a favorite. It was a very touching performance into which the congregation entered enthusiastically and wholeheartedly. As an observer and participant, I could not help but look around at the faces of the people as the song was being sung—and several verses of it were sung. The faces of the people were radiant with joy. It was an uplifting time for all of us, a time of celebration, a time when hearts were turned to Jesus, a time of worship within the Body of Christ. I dearly love this song and its sentiments.

I must tell you that I am a psychologist; and, among other things, that means I am a "people watcher." I am enthralled by people, and I lose myself in their actions and in their emotions. I study people and make educated guesses about them—that's what a psychologist must do. But beyond being a licensed psychologist with over thirty-five years experience teaching and counseling with people from many walks of life and of all ages, I served ten years as Professor of the Psychology of Aging at Baylor University's Institute of Gerontology. I guess that in the contemporary world of specialists, I am a gerontological psychologist.

I don't care for big words or big titles, but my concentration of recent years on the problems and functionings of mature people has caused me to be a "people watcher," especially of mature folk. I am trying hard not to use words like old, elderly, or aging because these words are so often used in a negative way.

Now, there was no doubt in anyone's mind that the question that was being posed in that little chorus focused on the hereafter, on a life in heaven, on a life with Jesus. It was evident that the congregation had their eyes fixed upon heaven and were thinking of the gates of eternity opening wide to receive them, that they might be forever at rest and at peace in the arms of the Lord. Their zeal, fervor, and commitment were evident in their voices and in their countenances. This is the beauty of a worship experience, particularly the musical—especially the singing.

Jesus said in John 14, "Let not your heart be troubled; ye believe in God, believe also in me. In my Father's house are many mansions; if it were not so I would have told you. I go to prepare a place for you. And if I go and prepare a place for you, I will come again, and receive you unto myself; that where I am, there ye may be also." (John 14:1-3) So, we Christians shall reside in that place He has prepared.

Living forever in heaven and holding onto that idea is the eternal hope of all Christians. Actually, I know deeply that it is not just a hope but a <u>reality</u> that brings untold joy to all of us within the

Christian heritage, within the Body of Christ. It is truly a biblical reality and one to which we may hold dearly and firmly.

Everlasting Life Beginning Now

Many things passed through my mind as I experienced this uplifting worship with this congregation. I knew then, as I know now, why we are admonished to gather ourselves together on the Lord's Day.

Again, as a psychologist, I am given to watching the expressions on the faces of people. I must do this in order to get inside the person I am counseling. I never intend to demean or discredit when I am so carefully observant.

It came to me during this time of singing that the older folk seemed more fervent, more joyful, more expectant in their rendering of the refrain, "I do," than even the youth of the church. I suppose we should not really be surprised about this. So many of the folk in the pews who were involved in the last third of their stay on this earth had fixed their eyes upon heaven, upon Jesus, upon the eternal promises of God that one day they would walk the streets of gold and would experience the joys of a reunion with the Lord. It is a favorite and generally an enjoyable time for Christians to think of the days beyond this present life. This is among the most uplifting thoughts a Christian can have. However, it is at least possible that fixing one's eyes on the hereafter may prohibit, inhibit, and limit the life that is now being lived.

Time Is in His Hand

I think that as I heard the refrain, "I do," and watched the faces, particularly of the older Christians, I overreacted to the possibility (maybe even the probability) that too many of the folk I was watching were so caught up in the forevermore, in the hereafter, in the promise of heaven that they were not as much in touch with present realities as they might have been. It has been my experience in personal psychotherapy with folk who have entered into their "golden years" that some of these people become isolated, withdrawn, introverted and look to the hereafter as an escape from experiences not altogether pleasant, sometimes filled with pain and sickness, sometimes fraught with frustrations brought about by health, family, and financial problems to mention only a few. In short, it has seemed to me on various occasions that many of my clients were leveling out their lives too soon and entering into an exclusive expectation of the hereafter too early. Is it possible that in concentrating on heaven we may fail to maximize the joys awaiting us right here on this beautiful planet? I believe it is possible. I also feel that we may become guilty of allowing our zeal in telling others about heaven to diminish our productivity as Christians. We may think and we may talk to others so exclusively about a heaven to be gained that we fail to think about either how hungry people are or how beautiful are the sunrises day by day right here on this beautiful planet.

Today, The First Day of the Rest of Your Life

The thought comes to me often that this eternal life of which we speak and toward which we yearn has already begun. Now is the day of salvation, now is the time to serve the Lord. Now we see through the dark glass—but at least we do see. Isn't it true that today, this day, is the first remaining day of your eternity? Eternity for you will not begin at death; it began the moment Christ entered your life. Christ came that we might have life. He does not teach us how to live in heaven. His constant message is hope of the kingdom to come but help for the kingdom at hand. We certainly should be exuberant about the reality of the heavenly abode, joyous of the eventuality of our reunion with Christ, and dedicated to the idea that all things will be new. Then, we shall see through the glass clearly, face-to-face.

18

There is a sentiment expressed in poetic form which says, "Take heaven now." The idea is that this life is so perfect (an unreasonable romantic notion) that there is no reason to wait for heaven. We already have it! The popular song declares, "Heaven can wait, just being here with you, breathing the air you do, heaven can wait." That is utter romantic nonsense even if it is an acceptable romantic song lyric.

No, you must keep looking forward to heaven because heaven does not begin when your everlasting life begins. Heaven, that glorious place where we will be able to sit at the feet of Jesus, is down the road just past the milestone of death.

But as Christians, we can think about heaven while we join with the Christ within us in joyfully embracing this life. Although this life is filled with frustrations, pain, and misery; it is also a time for joy—joy not just because we shall soon be home with Him, but joy promised in this life by a Christ who came that our joys might be full even before we get to heaven.

No, heaven is not now! Death is a milestone not on the way to everlasting life—it is a milestone on the road of everlasting life. It is our charge to make each new day a day of glorifying the God who gave us our eternal lives—lives that began when we were born again. There is no call for a third birth, only a second one, a birth into the kingdom of God. Search the scriptures, "For God so loved the world that He gave His only begotten son that whosoever believeth in Him should not perish but have everlasting life." (John 3:16)

In none of the scriptures which promise eternal life are there any indications that one must wait until death to lay hold on eternity. Eternity for each person is consummated with his acceptance of Jesus Christ as Lord and Savior. Granted, a few scriptures refer to houses and mansions eternal in the heavens, and so shall it be when we have passed the milestone of death which lies on the way of everlasting life. For Jesus is the way, Jesus is the life, and we possess Him and eternal life at the moment we are born again.

Growing in Joy

Growing older brings with it many problems. Some of us have failing health, some broken families, almost all experience either body aches, heartaches, or both. It should not be true that adversity is the glue that holds us to a joyful relationship with the Lord. On the other hand, adversity should never separate us from the love of nor from our joy in the Lord.

Is your joy in the Lord growing or waning? Are you allowing some feelings of despair related to your aging to get between you and your joy in the Lord? If the answer to either question is "yes," then you would do well to say, "Get thee behind me, Satan." That applies whether you feel that Satan is a personal demon intruding into your life or if you think of your own personal weaknesses as an evil force (Satan). The long and short of it is that as you move along the corridor of time toward a reunion with the Lord, your joy should become more and more full, even if sometimes your joy must be clouded by a film of physical or mental pain.

The Exceptional Rewards of Being an Older Christian

Gerontologists and psychologists, who are interested in the behavior of aging persons, have done many careful studies on the religious activities of older persons. Let's have a look at what they've found.

First, they have found that as people pass their seventieth birthdays, they begin to withdraw from human contact. Now mind you, these are averages and this may not describe your personal situation at all. But it is interesting to find that at least in England,

Canada, and the United States, folk begin to "disengage" from others beginning at about seventy.

And what about other age groups? Well, the researchers are finding that people remain about the same in social contacts (including worship and church-related activities) up to about age fifty. Then, between fifty and seventy, there is a shift toward more formal church activities together with reduced social contact of other types. Some people believe that the studies show that folk become stronger Christians as they grow older. Well, maybe. If you use religious activity as the only measuring stick, that is true.

On the other hand, some say that this increase in religious activities comes because the children are gone and people have more time for activities of all sorts including religion. I think it is only natural that people find more joy in the Lord when they are not as uptight about children, finances, and so forth. Don't you?

Careful research shows that the average person who is a Christian, demonstrates more and fuller joy in the Lord roughly between the fiftieth and seventieth year. Well fine, what happens then?

Research[1] [2] done with persons seventy or older indicates a decline in formal religious activities, and this is generally understood to mean that these folk are infirm or unable to attend worship services for one reason or another. However, there is after age seventy a large increase in "personal religious practices" such as prayer, Bible reading, and thinking about the everlasting kingdom[3]. Furthermore, there is an increase in dedication to "clean living" and most of all, to thinking of others and the "deep" meanings in life. Certainly, the

---

[1]Blazer D. and Palmore E. "Religion and Aging in a Longitudinal Panel." The Gerontologist. 16, pp. 82-84.
[2]Moberg, D.O. "Religiosity in Old Age." The Gerontologist. 5, pp. 78-87.
[3]Ainlay, S.C. and Smith, D.R. "Aging and Religious Participation." Journal of Gerontology. 39, pp. 357-363.

elderly have more time to do for and think of others, but that is not likely the full explanation. The evidence is that persons over seventy have less dedication to ritual, less concern for counting how often either they themselves or others perform the "required" religious practices. The evidence is that their personal relationship with God becomes more important to them. Their joys in their Lord become more personal and meaningful while also becoming more private.

As Christians become older, it should be evident that they find the chasm between this life and the next life much more narrow. They become more ready to make the short step from physical life to a new and different life. They step across the narrow chasm and joyfully pass another milestone on the road of everlasting life.

Universalizing Faith

In a beautifully expressed theory of religious faith, Dr. J. Fowler[4] outlines a development of faith into six stages. He calls the sixth and last stage "universalizing faith." It is clear that this last stage is seldom achieved by Christians under sixty years of age.

Fowler's belief is that only as we move into the 60-plus years do we begin to see through the glass somewhat more clearly. After passing the physical death milestone, of course, we will be able to see with total clarity. But it is the joy of older Christians to be able to grasp the "universalizing faith" principle. With this last stage of faith, Dr. Fowler says, "A seer (meaning one who sees) is able to perceive the unity behind contradiction . . . ."

The journey into faith is the ultimate journey. The young, no matter what their merits, cannot reach the zenith which belongs only to those who live long, who dedicate themselves in obedience to God's command, and who achieve full and final acceptance of God's plan.

---

[4]Fowler, J.W. Stages of Faith. Harper and Row, New York.

It is refreshing to see the "universalizing faith" principle in action. I often see it in nursing homes. Some people during their church-going days were bigoted, thinking that their particular church doctrine comprised ultimate truth. They did not open their arms and hearts to everyone regardless of race, color, or creed. I have seen evangelicals who throughout their lives deplored Catholicism reach out across that chasm when they came together in nursing homes. Even the Christian-Jewish dichotomy often vanishes with older people declaring, "We all worship the same Lord." Jewish residents are often anxious to attend protestant evangelical services in nursing homes. My wife, a pianist at these gatherings, tells me about Jewish women who sing the "Old Rugged Cross" with zeal and Protestant evangelicals who ask Catholic roommates to share religious symbols.

Does this show softening of brain tissue, incipient illnesses casting their hateful spells? Maybe sometimes it does. But for the most part, I think it illustrates godly love and a faith so deep that foolish sectarian divisiveness disappears in favor of universalizing and bonding faith. These elderly people are able to see through the darkened glass, and they see that the differences that have blocked Christian fellowship make no difference when one moves closer and closer to the milestone of death which lies along the way of everlasting life.

Will You Share With Me the Ultimate Victory?

Am I describing you in the above paragraph? Sadly, not all of us begin to see through the darkened glass. So many of you, being so deeply engrossed in your pain and despair of growing old along with your self-training in pessimism, miss the ultimate joy which can be yours only after you have grown into this last stage of faith. It makes no difference what we call it. "Universalizing faith" is just Dr. Fowler's phrase. He observed it in the lives of many older Christians and he had to call it something. You don't have to call it anything at all. Is this what the Bible means by achieving "sainthood"? It may be so.

It definitely is your choice and yours alone to grow into this unity with God, and you can do it under just <u>two</u> circumstances: 1) You must live long enough to achieve it. 2) You must keep your eyes joyfully upon the Lord, never allowing the despairing events of life to deter you nor to allow your own personal zest for life to wane.

I want to experience this kind of faith before I step across that narrow chasm into the next part of my everlasting life. Don't you?

Chapter 2

THE TERRIBLE TRAGEDY OF LIVING OLD AND DYING YOUNG

IT happens to everyone if he lives long enough. IT lurks on the horizon—even for those persons quite young. For many IT is a nightmare already come true. IT causes pain, demoralization, inability to breathe, and eventually a straight line on the oscillograph in ICU. IT begins in the twenties and thirties like a low, ominous rumble of thunder. At forty the rumble becomes more disquieting, and at fifty the storm breaks over many. No, IT isn't death, but there is no way to escape except to die. IT is called aging. The optimistic use the euphemism "the golden years" while the pessimistic with head down and despairing voices say, "IT is old age." Whatever IT is called, IT is inevitable for those who live. The message of this book will be clear and unyielding—IT can be very good, even great. IT does end in death according to the plan of God.

Old Age, a Gloomy or a Positive Reality?

If this horrible specter were death itself, then we could either fight it or accept it. Eventually, we would accept it, hopefully in the spirit of a risen Christ who declaimed, "O, death, where is thy sting? O, grave, where is thy victory?" (I Corinthians 15:55) Death has been conquered—old age has not.

Why do I begin this chapter with such a gloomy prologue? I do because all of these demeaning and despairing descriptions are actually, terrifyingly true right now for untold thousands of people around the globe including our own land of peace and freedom. Old age is an unspeakably bad scene for many people. Each of us is sharply aware that this is true because most have frail elderly among family and friends. And some of these ravages are inescapable under the most optimal circumstances; some of these assaults on the human body are invariably only the result of physically aging bodies and unavoidable disease wreaking havoc on minds and bodies. Ironically, the advancement of heroic medicine has brought to many people extra days and years of suffering and indignity, and this is likely a reason for the heightened awareness of the frightening specter of growing old. People know that they can be kept alive almost endlessly even when all tangible reasons for living are gone. The media finds mercy killing, euthanasia, and the agonies of Alzheimer's disease especially attractive. True, these things are newsworthy, but the overemphasis of the negative to the neglect of the satisfactions, health, and good fortunes of most aging persons is producing near hysteria among untold thousands. And unnecessarily so!

What You Believe About Aging Will Shape Your Living

I am convinced that the terrors of growing old are more mental and spiritual than physical. Many despised and devastating physical detractions of aging are avoidable, if not correctable. They can at least be dealt with in ways that preserve human dignity, positive thinking, and self-esteem.

If I thought for a moment that all or even most of the degradations of growing old had to remain with us, that these travails were meant to be, that these ravages were foreordained, that we must all surrender to the real and imagined horrors as they are described to us and lived out before us, I would at this moment lay down the pen. If I did not feel called by God to lead you out of the slough of despair and the night of your discontent as you approach the last one-third of your life expectancies, I wouldn't even try.

I refuse to believe that these horror stories do, should, or must represent the "facts of life" for all of us or even for most of us. Actually, I'm convinced these indignities are necessary only for a limited few of us. They do exist—these gruesome realities of pain and uselessness are all too real for many right now at this instance. On the other hand, these awful things may exist in the minds of many of us and demoralize us toward uselessness even if they never really happen. We have been brainwashed to believe the worst, and as a psychologist I am dedicated to the proposition that what has been erroneously learned and imagined can be unlearned to the elimination of darkness and relearned in the light of truth thereby helping us live life to its fullest. Meaningful life and helpful ministry to others is an attainable goal for people in wheel chairs—for any and all except a few frail and fragile persons who exist beyond the realms of human relating. Many who could find meaning in life do not, because no one has shown them how or encouraged them even to hope they can still be useful.

Growing Old or Dying Young

Either we grow old or we die young. Well, it may seem like a no-win situation. That is why I'm writing this book—I want to make you a winner.

We Christians look at death as inevitable and surely it is. Some of us are able to say that death gives meaning to life; death motivates us to live fully and sometimes joyfully. The Epicurean philosophers insisted, "Eat. drink, and be merry, for tomorrow you may die." Well, that's not exactly how we think about it, but when we think about it seriously, we know that God's plan of life and death must ultimately be the wise one. But growing old? That just shouldn't happen!

Someone has said, "Death is God's gift but old age is man's invention." Well, to say the least, old age is a state of mind, an attitude. Chronological age certainly doesn't convey what most people mean by old age. We all know old people of forty and young ones of ninety.

Why are people so appalled at growing old? If death is a gift, then how can one's latter years be all that bad? We are living at a time when an ugly image has encompassed getting old as never before. The sociologists call it ageism.

Young People Are the Champions

Ours is a youth-oriented society. Everything good is everything young. We worship lean and trim bodies, bright eyes, unwrinkled skin. Advertisers go for youthful models and those under forty try to emulate lifestyles of those in their twenties. For those of us in the last one-third of our lives, we are beginning to think very seriously about the inevitable and to shrink from it. Our thoughts shift from first looking at the media blitz applauding youth, to the media blitz showing older people as pitiable shells of non-persons who have few if any redeeming features.

The Myths of Aging

People over forty and particularly those approaching their fiftieth birthday are being hit over the head with many false and misleading ideas concerning their aging. This may be the first time in our history that people so young have had so much energy directed toward their own aging processes. Certainly, there are positive elements of this—it is good that people think ahead about their lives and plan constructively. The fact is, people who are looking ahead are devastated by the great number of myths concerning old age. Again, this is the youth generation—every emphasis is upon the youth, their music, their lifestyles, and the movement of some toward the drug culture. Seldom do people think about the sincere religiosity of many if not most of the young. But summarily, everyone thinks young is good while old is bad.

A large part of this myth referred to above involves the prototype of people approaching their sixtieth birthdays (even the fiftieth in the eyes of many). The prototype is of people who become slow-minded, dim-witted, forgetful, stooped, and bent with arthritis.

They become angry and disillusioned. According to the myths, bodies of older people are racked with pain and disease—indeed old age is seen as a disease itself. Other myths emphasize a disappearing sexuality, a high possibility of spending the last years of life in a nursing home, and the very great possibility that the last days will be spent in poverty. Many are convinced that the last years of life, perhaps the last thirty, will be meaningless and hopeless. Such people as these pitiable human shells are seen as non-human, vegetating, cranky, and burdensome.

Obviously, these hateful events are really happening to elderly people, but these descriptions do not represent the average situation for the great majority of us. To the contrary, we know that only about five percent of people over sixty-five live in nursing homes. The level of poverty among people over sixty-five is no higher than that for the population as a whole. Both men and women can and often do maintain active sexual lives into their nineties. Most elderly people have a satisfying life as demonstrated by reliable research[1]. But the minds of many, both young and old, refuse to envision the positive and are glued to the worst possible scenarios. And these worst scenarios are reinforced at every turn. Healthy, well-adjusted, happy, old people are not newsworthy. The media goes for the gruesome, the gory, and the heartbreaking stories of the little old bag ladies.

Aging Limitations

Government documents of the National Center for Health Statistics and the U.S. Bureau of the Census show the following: It is not until age 75 that over 50% of the population are physically or mentally limited in any way; and of that 50%, only 22% are limited to the point they cannot carry on a major activity. Even at 85, no more

---

[1]Palmore, E. Social Patterns in Normal Aging: Findings from the Duke Longitudinal Study. Duke University Press, Durham, N.C.

than 60% need the help of another person in personal care or home management activities.

The facts are, of course, that people are living to be much older than ever before. By the year 2000, the proportion of persons 55 and older will be 20% of the population. By the year 2010, this will jump to 25%, while those over 65 will represent about 15% of the population. By the year 2050, one-third of the population will be over 55, and 25% will be over 65. The "graying" of America is an undisputed future reality. It remains to be seen whether or not the "despairing" of America will occur also. It need not.

Life Expectancy

In 1900 the life expectancy was forty-seven years, while in the early 1990's life expectancy is 76 years for the longest living segment of our population, white females. There is a small variation from this life expectancy for males and for ethnics. Most elderly people continue to enjoy life, and there is an expressed high satisfaction with life among the elderly on average. These facts contradict the myths of aging that the elderly are miserable, sick, and depressed. Certainly, some are, but that need not be the outcome of your life.

It is a fact that young people at 40 years of age may expect to live for another thirty-five to fifty years. Statistics compiled by the American Council of Life Insurance show that a Caucasian female who is 40 in 1990 can expect 42 years of continued life. And that is the average. Many of us will live longer, some much longer. The time has come when one is considered to be middle-aged at 50 or 55, and a large portion of those who are in their seventies are still extremely active. It is a reality that sociologists have redefined the aging population breaking them into two groups: the first, those age 65 to 85, the second age 85 and up. It is generally agreed that the first of these groups, the young-old, may continue in productivity and activity until their 85th year. The situation for people older than age 85 is as it

THE TERRIBLE TRAGEDY OF LIVING OLD AND DYING YOUNG

must be, one which embraces fast decline and death. Indeed, some authorities predict that not many years hence, 85 will be the average life expectancy and that almost everyone will live to that age. But with that age one must expect a rapid decline. True, some people live to be 100 and over while a few live to be 115. Actually, 115 years is said to be the end of the life span for the human and that no human will ever live longer. Even this idea has been attacked, and it is suggested that with breakthroughs involving the immunological system of the human, the 115 year life span for humans may be extended. The fastest growing segment of our population at this time is those people over 85, and it is easily seen that the population will from this point grow older on average until life expectancy approaches the life span. Certainly, we must not be guilty of suggesting that living longer is the ultimate goal. Living better longer may or may not be. It depends on what we value.

The Nation's Power Base Will Shift

There is a reason for the media blitz about aging. While the blitz itself is usually hurtfully negative, it does give us valuable information. Because of shifting population trends, the baby boomers of the forties and fifties are passing or approaching their fortieth birthdays now and will soon be among the young-old. And what will that mean? It will mean to a large extent what we want it to mean and what we make it mean. Hopefully, it will mean that the nation's power base, the command generation, will shift to the young-old group.

It is understandable that people who are relatively young are becoming confused and anxious about the years which lie ahead. Some are worrying about drugs and rampant crime, fearing they'll never live to grow old. Others are worrying about whether they will have any way of surviving if they do make it. Will the Social Security check be there, or will the system be bankrupt? Can I save enough to make it when prices are skyrocketing? Can I get my kids raised? Through college?

But probably the main worries are more personal. What's going to happen to me? Will I be happy? Will I even have a reason to live? Some would say that the answer for these people is to tell them to trust the Lord. He gave them all these extra years, and He'll see them through. But some along with me feel that trusting the Lord requires that we put feet under that trust and do something. We are right!

Early Retirement

And then, as strange as it may seem, every active force around us seems to be encouraging early retirements, some as early as fifty. Those who are in very stressful positions look forward to retiring early. Even though mandatory retirement has been raised to seventy and may soon be abolished altogether, the records show that very few people are staying on the job until age seventy. Early retirement seems to be the rule rather than the exception.

One cannot but be amazed to think of the difference between retiring at 65 in 1935, the year when Social Security set that age as the age for getting old, and retiring at 50 or 55 in the nineties. Actually, from 1935 until 1990 there has been a gain in life expectancy of 11 1/2 years so that it would make sense to believe that a person who is 76 1/2 is really at the same point in his life as was the person who was 65 in 1935.

Living Abundantly

From this we can easily see how unbelievable it is that people would retire at 50 in 1990, that is to say disengage completely from work and life. The reality is that by disengaging at 50, they may spend 35 to 50 years in limbo. There may come a time when a person spends as much time after leaving the major job as he does before he starts on his vocational journey. The people who are now in their fifties have the best part of their lives ahead.

While those of us who are in our seventies reasonably know about these realities, it is not easy for those of you who are fifty to grasp the reality of these changes. Actually, you could spend years in helpless and hopeless dismay as you try desperately to get your feet under you, getting your lives in order so that you enjoy your "golden years."

I am very anxious to have people who are 50-plus read this book. It is a pity that people at whatever age are unable to maximize their lives. It is a sad reality that those who are approaching what is generally referred to as aging must hurdle many barriers and change a lot of attitudes before they can get in the mood to move forward productively into the last one-third to one-half of a life which could be full, rich, and meaningful—actually more so than ever before.

The Tragedy of an Unwanted Life

I remember Aunt Sue and Uncle Joe. They were my favorites when I was a teenager. They treated me special. I went fishing a lot with Uncle Joe. And Aunt Sue made the best blackberry pies in the world. At the same time, she could be a little contrary at times. But not for very long at a time, thank goodness.

These two devoted Christians and beloved family members were about seventy when I was about fifty. I remember something being said on their fiftieth wedding anniversary. It had to do with their future.

Uncle Joe, hale and hearty, vowed he'd live to be one hundred. He even joked about what kind of woman he wanted as a second wife. Aunt Sue vowed that was all right with her. With her arthritis she would not be long for this world. She said, "I hope the good Lord takes me home soon; I've had enough of this world." She really meant it, too.

What happened? We buried Aunt Sue a month ago. She was ninety-two. The last twenty-two years of her life were spent in abject misery for Aunt Sue and for everyone who came in contact with her. She whined her way through twenty years, and never a day passed that she didn't express the hope that the Lord would take her that very night. She was a virtual invalid for the last ten years, and it seemed she caused everyone, especially one of her daughters, unreasonable and unnecessary misery.

"But what about Uncle Joe?" you are asking. Maybe I should have told you that first. He died of a heart attack at age seventy-two. Uncle Joe didn't live the robust life of a hundred years he so fondly expected. Is that so terrible? No, the fact that he wanted to live so fervently wasn't important at all after he died.

But Aunt Sue! Dear old soul. She hated every minute of her twenty years alone. She never wanted to live them in the first place, but she did live them. All of this has always seemed such a tragedy to me. But it was God's plan.

Now, I am seventy-two. I'd rather it was for me like it was for Uncle Joe, but I'm going for the one hundred if He'll let me.

Oliver Wendell Holmes, the famous poet of yesteryears, made the following statement when he was 80 years of age, "There are two kinds of people who live to be 70 years of age. The first kind expect to live until they're 90, and the second kind expect to die. For those who expect to live to be 90 and who die it makes no difference; for those who expect to die at 70 and live to be 90, it is hell." Without apology for Mr. Holmes's language, he had a point to make which is very powerful. The amazing thing is that Mr. Holmes was 80 years of age about 50 years ago when he made this statement. In these final few years of the 20th century, we would have to revise a statement like that to say, "A person who gets to be 90 comes in two types, etc." But the reality is that the sentiments which Mr. Holmes expressed for people who were age 70 in his time applies to even younger groups of people today.

We might with total candor say, "Some people approach their 50th birthdays expecting to become useless and miserable while some expect to live to be happy and useful until they are 100. For those who live to be 100 and who are miserable for 50 years, that is unthinkable."

Chapter 3

AGING, DEFEATS AND VICTORIES— SPIRITUAL REALITIES

The topic of human life is the most deeply spiritually-laden one which exists in this world and that which is to come. One need not belabor the appropriateness of aging as a spiritual concern. Christ has said, "I am the way , the truth, and the life." (John 6:11) If life itself is spiritual, being by definition that which not only is of God but that which is God, then can an effort to enhance life, to magnify it, to make it useful, or to make it joyous be less than spiritual? Speaking of the little children, Christ said, "Suffer the little children to come to me, and forbid them not: for of such is the kingdom of heaven." (Mark 10:14) God's all-embracing glorification of human life reaches from Elizabeth's joy song because of her knowledge through the Holy Spirit that her friend Mary was carrying the immaculate conception within her, to Christ's death to achieve our own everlasting lives.

Spiritual Realities

Are you wondering, "Is this a spiritual book? Is this written by a Christian psychologist? He seems to have at least a nodding acquaintance with the Scriptures; he speaks of Christ and His teachings."

"But isn't it true," you say, "that while human life is a spiritual concern, the degradations of old age are just physical realities with no spiritual significance? Must we not suffer the torments of the damned in this life in order to inherit the kingdom of heaven? Are not old age, senility, and pain simply and logically biological and social realities all of which were designed in the mind of God to get us ready for the releasing power of death and to project us into the everlasting kingdom?" Yes, my friend, it is true. But no, my dearest friend, it is untrue. Can the answer to this or any question be both "yes" and "no"?

Emphatically yes, all of life is sacred and any aspect of a glorification, a celebration, or a prolongation of meaningful life on this earth is a spiritually laden proposition. Emphatically no! One's place in heaven is not related to the amount or length of pain, isolation, abuse, or meaninglessness one may suffer before one's death. Jesus suffered on the cross, and through his suffering, we all were redeemed. ". . . with his stripes we are healed." (Isaiah 53:5)

On the other hand, we are called upon to take up the cross and follow Him. The Christian knows that much suffering has supreme meaning and does not always ask for the silver lining. The Christian is often called upon to suffer for His name's sake. Tertullian has said, "He who fears to suffer cannot be His who suffered." And from I Peter 3:17, "For it is better, if the will of God be so, that ye suffer for well doing, than for evil doing."

Is Suffering For Its Own Sake Redemptive?

The point I want to make is that suffering for suffering's sake has nothing to commend it, but suffering for the glory of God affirms His redemptive suffering. One is required to glorify and celebrate his life with or without pain. Adversity, pain, and frustration, in and of themselves, assure nothing, least of all the pleasure of God.

Christ opposes useless and senseless human suffering, alienation, and abuse, and did so until His earthly end when, from the cross turning to John, he said, "Behold thy mother." (John 19:27) We take some liberty in believing that John understood Christ to be saying, "Cherish her. Her life is yours to love and serve."

God Is No Respecter of Persons

Our society, youth-oriented as it is, constantly devalues the elderly. In a broad sweeping way, society values youth and depreciates the elderly. But God is no respecter of persons! Chronological age has no meaning in terms of human value, or in terms of the worth or the dignity of the person.

So often we hear in sermon, speech, or song that the elderly have earned the right to reverence. It is said that we have served our time, have fathered and mothered the young, have contributed to the economic stability of the nation, have fought the nation's wars, and on and on. Without wishing to be irreverent toward the elderly (of which I am one), I must tell you that I don't think we (as a group or individually) deserve any such lionization. We did what we did out of motives not always as pure as the driven snow. We were just doing our jobs, rearing our children, and making a living. We deserve no special credits for what we have done or are doing, and we should desire no sympathies for our number of years or our aging bodies.

Don't Believe All You Hear

At the risk of appearing a bit pugnacious, I must tell you that all this praise coming as it does from our youth, our politicians, our ministers, and even our peers should not become a centerpiece of our lives. What we have done we have done. I am afraid all this gushing has hidden agendas. "You've done well, old man (woman). You'll never know how much we appreciate you; we revere you. Thank you very much. Now, go gently into the dark night. Approach thy death like one who lies down to pleasant dreams."

Don't you recognize most of this as basically a con job pulled off by con artists who do not even know that they are conning us? They are following the cliches of the past often with good sentiments, not realizing that with the increase in life expectancy and myriad other factors, we have more to offer than sedate advice. We are not dim-witted and decrepit. Many of us are the middle-aged folk during the last years of this century, for middle age is now considered to be about fifty to fifty-five. Our value and worth, aside from the fact that all human life is to be cherished, is as great as we choose to make it! Not only has our value as persons <u>not</u> decreased with age, but our value as contributors very well might even yet increase.

As I review the statements immediately above, I think I have indeed been overly pugnacious. The generational gaps are real. However, it behooves young and old alike to remember that we are all in the same family of God. There should be no animosity between generations, and we must do everything possible to minimize differences.

A recent Harris poll shows the following as quoted by Kingston et al.:

1. More than four-fifths of family members aged 18 to 24 run errands for parents or grandparents and help them when someone is ill.

2. Even people aged 80 and over continue to provide support to younger generations in their families, with 57 percent helping out when someone is sick and 23 percent running errands.[1]

There Is a Reason

The hidden agenda behind so much of this is to ease the 50-plus person into retirement, and to grease the skids for their removal from the workplace. Do you know that fully functioning persons at fifty are being pressured out of their rightful roles as movers and shakers in our worlds of business, service industries, manufacturing, and high technology?

---

[1] Kingson, Eric R., Hirshorn, Barbara A. and Cornman, John M. <u>Ties That Bind</u>. Seven Locks Press. Washington, D.C. 1986.

I want to say to the baby boomers especially: "In a few years you will be the senior boomers and for the first time in human history you will have dwindling population groups on both sides of you." The nation will collapse unless the elderly prepare themselves for meaningful work in their later years. Laws against mandatory retirement to the contrary, people are being shunted out of active lives earlier and earlier. Actually, they don't take much shunting. People in this respect become their own worst enemies.

At this point, let us close this short chapter with a reaffirmation of human worth. All human persons are worthy because the Lamb is worthy. He has given us His worthiness by becoming our brother. And our worth does not diminish with age. In the human sense, it never diminishes; in the marketplace sense, it need not diminish for a very long time unless we want it to. In terms of national survival, we dare not concede a diminishing value for the elderly. Our worth can continue, it must continue, it will continue!

Chapter 4

THE BLESSINGS OF OLD AGE

The hoary head is a crowning glory, if it be found in the way of righteousness. (Proverbs 16:31)

God made old age blessing. The Bible says, "Honor thy father and thy mother that your days may be long upon the earth." (Exodus 20:12) And Timothy 5:17 says, "Let the elders be counted worthy of double honor." I am writing this book to remind you that God did not require pain, depression, or guilt as a condition for a life after this life. Suffering and anguish in this life are the results of sin, and not as a means by which God assures us of a heavenly abode. Belief in His son is all that is required for everlasting life! God applauded longevity as a virtue and a gift; and although He wrote in His master plan that every man is given once to die, over and over He glorified long life as both blessing and obligation.

At age ninety-nine, Abram covenanted with God that he should have a son by Sarah (then eighty years of age) and that Abram would become the father of many nations. This is a startling testimony to the fact that God is here for you and for me right now regardless of our ages.

Victorious Living Until Death

Chronological age should have nothing to do with victorious living. You can live in victory no matter where you may be found along the corridor of time. This book is devoted to victorious living in the last one-third of your life on this earth. A life that is not victorious, joyful, and meaningful is an affront to God and His plan for you. God cherished for us a long life so that we might joyfully glorify Him. Are you bemoaning your adversities because you are growing old? God will not be happy about that and neither will you!

I am not trying to make you feel guilty if you are depressed about growing older. In the long run, you are entitled to make the decision about your life. No one can make decisions about how you are going to see your life except you yourself. But if you are going to insist on feeling sorry for yourself, you should not read this book.

I know I shall die. I will be given once to die as is every person. But this book is not about dying; that comes naturally. Rather, this book is about living, and I hope that as you read it, you will never forget that death is our common heritage. Do not set your eyes on death; that is a mistake. Own your mortality, just as you own your immortality. Then, turn your eyes with me to life, turn your eyes upon Jesus who is life.

God's Plan is in Our Best Interests

Are you wishing to change God's plan? Well, you are circumventing His intentions if you see death exclusively as the great enemy of life and if because of this you do not live fully, thus affirming His gift of abundant life. Please remember, you are already well into your eternal life. God's plan is not ours to question, but we may be reminded that God's plans do sometimes change. He changed His mind about destroying Sodom upon Abraham's pleading. Has He changed His mind about human life expectancy? I believe that through His marvelous gift of science, He has extended our life expectancy beyond the three score and ten of which the Psalmist speaks. It is happening, so how can it be other than His plan—a plan of life unchangeable in some ways; yet, in His wisdom, changeable in others.

The elders of the New Testament were not only revered, they were constantly called upon for wisdom and for action. Peter said, "The elders which are among you I exhort . . . feed the flock . . . not by constraint but willingly; not for filthy lucre, but of a ready mind. Neither as being lords over God's heritage but being ensamples to the flock." (I Peter 5:1-4) And to the young he exhorted, " . . . submit yourself to the elder." (I Peter 5:5)

It is clear from the Bible that all of us who may be elderly are not elders in the sense of being specially singled out as religious leaders. It is clear that there were those appointed as elders among the congregation of Israel. This practice continued into the New Testament church, wherein men of good report were designated as elders in the church. In modern congregations the term elder is used in several ways to designate authority and responsibility, resulting in positions of influence and leadership.

Biblical Admonitions to the Elderly

Even so, it behooves us as members of a select generation of older people to hear what God through Joshua, Peter, and the apostles said to and about the elders. The most common phrase used in addressing the elders was, "I exhort thee." From this and from multitudes of other references we may know that the elders were seen as people of wisdom, of courage, and of vision. There is seldom a sentiment toward the elders or the elderly of, "rest upon thy laurels and take thine ease." It was, for the most part, "Teach the young, care for the widows and orphans, do this, arrange that this be done." True, the elders grew old and faint; even as Joshua "waxed old and stricken in age," so did they. But the record is clear, the elders were "doers" and not only "hearers" of the word. Disengagement from useful activity occurred only when they, like Joshua, were "stricken."

Old age is a time of blessedness. One moves constantly closer to his destiny with death, but he need not move away from his active involvement with life until "stricken unto death." Old age is a time for being blessed and a time for blessing others. It is not a time for withdrawal, pessimism, or being marginally involved with life.

A Great Time of Life

The "golden years" need not be a euphemism. There is much to commend the last one-third of our lives. It should be a fact that because of our wide experiences, we have really learned how to live. True, many of our problems are very much with us yet. We have aging parents to whom we have become as parents while we ourselves are parents of our own struggling offspring. Our children and grandchildren choose unwisely and behave in ways not to make us proud. These are among the negatives.

On the positive side, we should have settled into some comfortable niches. For some of us, financial security has arrived (relatively, at least). Most of us have learned to manage our worlds as opposed to being managed by the forces around us. At least it is possible, even probable, that we have overcome some neuroticisms; we have stepped into life's ongoing flow. We know that getting upset over minor hassles doesn't solve anything, and we hopefully have achieved a more "laid back" attitude. We worry about the things about which something can be done, and we do what needs to be done. So far as things outside our control are concerned, we are learning to let these things just slip by.

I know the above is likely an overly-optimistic statement. However, it does seem that we ought to have achieved these calmer ways of seeing and of being in our worlds. At long last many of us are really hearing God through His word, "But my God shall supply all your need according to his riches in glory by Christ Jesus." (Philippians 4:19) and, "God is our refuge and strength, a very present help in trouble."(Psalm 46:1)

The Browning Sentiment

The poet, Robert Browning, said it convincingly in Rabbi Ben Ezra:

"Grow old along with me"
The best is yet to be,
The last of life, for which the first was made;
Our times are in his hand
Who saith, "A whole I planned,
Youth shows but half; trust God; see all, nor be afraid!"

As beautiful as this sentiment is, it is yet lacking. Indeed, there is not a two-part life, youth and age. It is only one life, and to separate it into two even for sentiment's sake leaves something amiss.

I could hope that I could live my life only as the "whole He planned" with no looking back, only forward. With David, the psalmist, I would say, "With long life will I satisfy him, and show him my salvation." (Psalm 91:16)

Chapter 5

CHRONOLOGICAL AGE IS SECONDARY— ATTITUDES ARE PRIMARY

For as he thinketh in his heart, so is he. (Proverbs 23:7)

Martha Greer was seventy-eight years old last week. She and her husband Gary built a life together which stretched to fifty-three years of marriage, five children, and a heady state of affluence plus a fine reputation in the Christian community.

Something unbelievable happened to Gary. Some said it was sickness, others that he had become demon-possessed. Whatever went wrong, Gary purportedly fell in love with a much younger woman—a gold digger, most of Martha's church friends said. Gary started liquidating assets several years ago. In ways most would have thought legally impossible, Gary managed jointly held assets and community property in which Martha had half interest in such a way that most of their money got squirreled away in bank accounts in his own name.

Then Gary filed for divorce. Under the no-fault divorce laws, Martha could do nothing. Gary got his divorce with no problem, and Martha, a lady accustomed to affluent living, was left with virtually nothing. Gary was generous enough to leave her the family home, but as little money as his legal chicanery permitted. He married his child sweetheart, as the church ladies called her.

Needless to say, Martha Greer was crushed. She had no work skills, few assets, and a long, lonely life ahead. Absolutely no one would have predicted that all these indignities would befall this fine Christian lady.

This is an appropriate way to say that the only truly predictable thing about life is change. Changes are having profound influences on the lives of all citizens, especially upon their future hopes and possibilities. Inflation, high interest rates, tightening job markets, and

S&L scandals are playing economic havoc. Eroding morality, crime, and the breakdown of families are causing many to be amazed at the frightening morass of societal change.

No group of individuals is more threatened by change than are we, the maturing and aging. Older Americans are becoming pawns in the economic and social games being played out in this changing world. Older Americans are faced with great challenges to maintain their senses of personhood, of intrinsic worth, of meaningful existence and of contribution to the directions this changing world will go. They must reorder their thinking, their attitudes, their ways of seeing and reacting to their worlds. Sadly, however, there is much apathy, malaise, and self-pity among maturing citizens. Too many are resigning themselves to lives of hopelessness and gloom. We must try to do something about this! We all know being Christian does not remove us from the threat of catastrophe.

Anything Except the Status Quo

It just cannot be allowed to continue this way. And a revolution is in the making to turn it around. The world needs to wake up to the reality that older citizens who have reared their children (or at least passed through that span of life), who have carved out for themselves a place of hopeful financial security, and who have known this country in its strength and world prominence will not sit idly by and allow either the status quo or worse. While they see their advancing years and the state of the nation as stressful and frightening, they are beginning to marshal their forces toward throwing off the shackles with which they have been bound, intimidated, and made powerless. Older Americans must come to know that we have the power to make our own lives meaningful and rewarding and that we have a tremendous stake in the future of this country and in the ongoing Kingdom of God. Older Americans are not going to take it anymore—we have been sold short, and we are tired of it.

If what you have just read seems overly assertive, it is. Such an organized, coherent set of attitudes among our peers really hasn't jelled yet. There is great need to dramatize the realities and to solidify the forces that are simmering but haven't yet boiled. The disturbing evidence is that a majority of us are viewing the possibilities of our lives as static and uninviting. But we aren't yet doing very much about it.

"Old age is a bad scene, we'll wind up penniless and in a rest home," one despairing older person told me recently. To which I did, and do, and must say, "It could be true, especially if you expect it to be; but it isn't necessarily so." Our chief enemy is that we believe what we hear. We endorse what we hear, we help create what we hear, and we often revel in the prediction of our own sorry state. We have listened too often and too long to the prophets of doom insofar as aging is concerned. The years of maturity, the so-called senior years, and even old age have been seriously misrepresented as being decadent, passive, and without virility. But age is really not the principal factor in deterioration, and that can be proved. Fast-paced change has cast a pall on all of us, but new information is showing the falsity of earlier suppositions. The picture that has been painted is false; it is scurrilous; it is inaccurate. We must reassess the accuracy of the myths of aging and reexamine our attitudes towards ourselves in order to see to what extent our attitudes constitute the real problem.

Age Is Not Necessarily a Factor

Aging has become a tremendously popular concern for researchers and writers during the last few years. Research ad infinitum has been done with aging subjects to determine whether or not the conditions popularly associated with aging really are true for them. The results are that to a large extent, many of the negative features ascribed to old age are myths. It is obvious, of course, that everyone grows older, and it would be ridiculous to hope that advancing years will leave any of us untouched by the ravages of time. Indeed, we may be assured that old age will bring very hurtful changes—there will never be an argument about that.

On the other hand, many changes which have seemed unavoidable for us have not happen as predicted. For instance, studies on intelligence of aging persons have shown that there has been great misinformation concerning intellectual and cognitive functioning as people grow older. (See Chapter Eleven.)

All aging persons have been thrown together by some researchers into a single group to achieve statistics about the "average aging person." You and I do not need to be like the "average," and so we must take statistics about the capabilities of aging persons with a "grain of salt." Aging persons change in intelligence differentially person by person, and those changes are not always or even typically damaging until the onset of terminating illness or other catastrophe.

Research has been done on memory, on speed of performance of both physical and mental tasks, on physical degeneracy of organ systems, on sexual capabilities, and other factors ad infinitum. New revelations have exploded many myths on the one hand, and on the other have tended to promise to the aging person a rich and rewarding life where before there had been nothing but gloom. In part, these encouragements are the products of broad-based changes in the world about us such as improved health. It is obvious that these changes can be credited to our changing attitudes about aging in general and about ourselves in particular. If it is allowed to go unchallenged that we are degenerating at the rate the myths suggest and if we older persons have the expectancy of these events, then all these things will formulate a self-fulfilling prophecy. Indeed, this is the way it seems to be working out. If we believe we are degenerating all that much with age, we will degenerate.

We must examine the forces in our society which have cast a pall of depression upon many of us who have passed our fiftieth, sixtieth, seventieth, or even eightieth birthdays. We need to assess realities and then determine that the years ahead will be the most productive of all. We must learn that the viewpoints concerning old age as they exist in some minds are erroneous, hurtful, and sometimes virtually vindictive.

In Numbers There Is Strength

Because of the recent trends in birth rates, we will soon reach the point when over 25 million citizens will be 65 years of age or older, almost 12% of the population. These numbers emphasize the need we have to properly and accurately assess the situation and then to assert the positive factors of our lives. There is little doubt that society, often with our own consent, has sold its older citizens out—has sold them old. Many forces in this ambiguous world have caused us to respond with depression and sometimes with horror to our aging process. For instance, the largest incidence of suicides is among white males over 65 years of age. However, many persons of advancing years embrace their lives as extremely meaningful and live out their lives with a sense of purpose, accompanying happiness, and usefulness to society. The mature years in many ways could be happier and more productive than many intermediate spans of life. They will be our best years if we are determined to make them so!

The nation can ill afford the loss of strength and virility that is represented in a population of 25 million people. Indeed, with up to 12% of persons being 65 or older, we will find that we are the center of power insofar as the welfare of the nation is concerned. We represent a large amount of the consummate wisdom needed to bring the nation forward, to work out our economic problems, and to insure a better life for generations to come. The political clout of a senior voting bloc is destined to become a mover and shaker in the years ahead, but only if we get our act together.

The Methuselah Syndrome

Unless our attitudes change drastically, we shall never be able either to utilize or maximize our power. We are experiencing a collective attitude toward and among our peers which may well be called the Methuselah Syndrome. Various forces in society are causing us to feel old, to act old, and to lose meaning for our lives simply because these forces are manipulators. In many instances, the forces which are selling us out as useless and as having lives without meaning are doing so with some degree of maliciousness. In other cases, the intent is not at all malicious, but hurtful nonetheless. The media is exploiting us in terms of advertising schemes to inveigle us into feeling many of the "pains" of old age. We are being coerced by the get-rich-quick schemes of entrepreneurs to buy various products which are prescribed by advertisers as corrective for the seldom inevitable degenerative functions we are supposed to endure. The message, for instance, is that to be sixty is to be arthritic.

Mr. Mason was ninety-seven years old when he joined the talk group at the nursing home. He listened intently while Ruth talked about how everyone can help others. After the session he asked, "How can I help others, Ruth? I just don't know what I can do."

"You are a Christian, aren't you, Mr. Mason?" Ruth asked.

"I sure am!" Mr. Mason replied enthusiastically.

"Well, then why don't you witness every day to someone in this home. I believe they'll listen to you. You've been a salesman all your life, you know."

"I think I'll do it," he said. And he did. He didn't miss a day witnessing until he died a year later. He was happy, and he was a champion. What's more, he knew and he felt he was important right up to the time when he went quietly to sleep and didn't awake until heaven's door swung quietly shut behind him.

The Political System Doesn't Always Help

Political forces have constituted a disservice to citizens with demeaning programs which, while possibly well-intentioned, have produced a population of persons who feel older than they need feel. The Social Security system, while exceedingly helpful, has been guilty of forcing age upon people who otherwise would be more productive for many years. For instance, it was a political ploy to make it possible to retire early at age sixty-two. Rules stipulating that we can earn only limited amounts without penalties against our Social Security checks are unfair. Mandatory retirement systems have been hurtful to some of us, and various aspects of the legal system are encouraging the able elderly to release their holds on meaningful and ongoing work sooner than is necessary.

The system has encouraged the accumulation of wealth only to be handed down to children who do not endorse either the work ethics or other values held by us who have created the wealth. Forces of organized religion, without really meaning to do so, have brought us to a state of looking fervently for the releasing power of death while having thirty or forty years left to maximize our lives. We are being robbed of a meaningful present in being urged to look compulsively and exclusively to the eternal future. Remember! We are into our futures right now. We are living our everlasting lives right now, and some of us are making a self-deprecating mess of this part of our everlasting lives.

We can throw aside these depressing images and break the shackles of the Methuselah Syndrome with which we have been bound. We must refuse to knuckle under to the forces which are robbing many of us of our senses of meaning, happiness, and productivity because of negative views of aging.

The Spans of Life

Psychoanalyst Erik Erikson[1] during the 1950's set forth an eight-stage span of life which moves from infancy to mature age and death. Erikson's eighth stage is called integrity vs. disgust and despair. Erikson indicates that at retirement age (He indicates fifty-five as the usual age of beginning this span.), we enter into either a sense of integrity or a sense of despair. If we choose integrity, then we accept our lives and "grow old gracefully." The integrity of which Erikson spoke seemed to be the epitome of everything good for the older citizen. Certainly, it was much better to gain integrity and see our lives in positive lights than it would be to sink into despair and despondency, thus creating misery for ourselves and for those around us. Erikson's sense of integrity has many positive features reflecting the era of the fifties in which it was formulated. The concept of integrity is useful and it has a positive ring to it, but it will not get the job done for us during this last decade of the twentieth century. We are living so much longer now that we need new ways of looking at reality.

The New Eighth Span

A new eighth span of life must be added. I am issuing a call to you to reenergize the years of your maturity into a way of living that emphasizes continuing activity. The changing world, increased life expectancy, and dozens of fresh new forces demand that we visualize a

---

[1] Erikson, Erik. Identity, Youth and Crisis. W.W. Norton. New York. 1968.

new eighth span of forceful and meaningful participation in life. We need Erikson's concept of integrity well enough, but integrity must be pushed forward into a ninth span, which requires us to demand a new level of involvement with life for our many remaining years.

Let us be honest. We know very well that a vast majority of post-retirement persons have not chosen a continued, exciting involvement. Instead, they have become victims of despair. And it will continue to be so unless we insist on exercising the realistic rights and privileges which belong only to those who demand them.

Nursing homes are filled with persons who could be productive. How many persons are vegetating in nursing homes only because they have nothing to do and no other place to go? We do not know, but we can guess that there are many.

Few persons choose depression and loss of vitality because they really want it that way. But in our world of throw-away goods, we also have throw-away people. Ageism as a societal problem will be solved only if we who are being relegated into meaninglessness will become aroused, will stop listening to false prophets, and will demand and obtain what rightfully is ours. Disengagement theory holds that older people fare better if they disengage from work and life to save their waning strength against the certain assaults of disease and death. This may have seemed appropriate, satisfying, and the ultimate of everything good to the maturing person of thirty years ago. But not now! We may seriously question whether or not we can with impunity surrender our command when there is no one more capable than we. We know beyond a shadow of a doubt that disengagement from life serves no advantage. We know that disengagement brings weakness, not strength.

The span of life has long been a useful metaphor. But spans of life are reshaping themselves. These so-called spans have described the journey from cradle to grave. But as with any bridge over time, troubled waters or chasms, the bridge over life may be described as a single span or as a group of interlocking spans. And with emerging realities, the bridge needs rebuilding to take into account the many years that have been added to human life expectancy. True, there will be an end. But during the last decade of the twentieth century, life's ending should not be conceptualized as beginning with some arbitrarily-set event or chronological age. We must realize the truth—the best part of life on this planet lies ahead for many if not most of us!

I am convinced that old age is basically a state of mind and that our degeneracy until terminating illness is more myth than fact. This book will continue to try to encourage you to find ways and means for maximizing your lives.

Solutions

How can we escape the Methuselah Syndrome? How can we muster the courage to challenge the forces that are trying to make us feel old? Many if not most of the elements which bring about breakdown in the latter years are controllable. For instance, nutrition has been shown to be remarkably potent in keeping older persons active and productive. Good health, while a reasonable goal of any person at any time of life becomes an imperative for the aging person. Great attention must be given to the continuing search for the helpful factors of nutrition, exercise, surgery, medication, and self-management which can keep us alive, alert, and productive. The health factor cannot be overemphasized. Many rules for the maintenance of health and vigor are easily available including diets, exercise programs, and self-care relating to our principal enemies—cancer, heart disease, diabetes, and arthritis.

Time Wasted Is Time Lost

True, older persons have been sold short by the political and legal systems. But laws can be changed; regulations can be put in place in some instances and abolished in others. The statuses of older persons can be made secure by appropriate political and legal actions designed to protect and enhance the lives of persons as they enter into this eighth span of life. To a large extent, this has been done through the Older Americans Act. In a sense the ball is in our court. If we don't shape up and make the effort, we will have no one to blame but ourselves.

We must, of course, grow older—time is ultimately the great enemy of earthly life; but there are many enemies that can often be defeated once they are recognized and confronted. It is certainly conceded that we shall never be able to defeat time; but on the other hand, we know that time wasted is time lost and that we need not allow ourselves to feel half dead when we can be totally alive. Isn't it abysmally sad that people are giving up their lives at 50, 60, and 70? Yes! Especially when they are living physically into their 80's and 90's!

Continuity

Somehow we must let those in their 30's know that life doesn't grow sour as the body grows old. Obviously, we cannot convince the young until we convince ourselves. We must remember that what we do now to enlarge the scope of mature life presages what happens to our children and grandchildren. We must be role models for the young; for, if we do not, they will not know how to slip productively into their own golden years. We must become the pioneers for a new wilderness; we must wrest meaningfulness and productivity from this unexplored domain. We are entering an era where the average person will live 85 years as opposed to 47 years in 1900 and 76 in 1990. We have never been here before. Those of us now in our late maturity must show the way.

And why must we? Simply because there is no one else who can accomplish for God and for our country what we can accomplish. And no one else can chart the uncharted. We were the "command generation" of the 60's and 70's, and there is no one to take over the command right now. But it is not only that we must continue; it is good for us to continue, and we <u>can continue</u>. We must make the world understand that active, meaningful, productive life does not necessarily end or even wane at 50, at 60, at 70, or even at 80. Most of all, we must be the bearers of salvation and must make others understand that God has given all of us extra, eventful years on this planet. We are just spending a few more years of our everlasting lives on earth. Thanks be to God that our extra years on earth take nothing away from our time in heaven. It's everlasting after all!

<u>Champions</u>

Who among us should be counted as champions? Are they only found among those continually healthy, virile, fully-functioning individuals who continue their outstanding successes into their 70's, 80's, and 90's? Is a President of the United States functioning exceptionally well in his 60's and 70's a champion? Is a 78-year-old heart surgeon working fourteen-hour days in critical, life-threatening emergencies a champion? Is a 92-year-old minister, who is still effectively fulfilling world-wide evangelism, a champion? Of course they are! But so are wheel chair victims if their attitudes toward life are wholesome and expectant.

Most of Us Can Be Champions

Neugarten et al.[2] have described the "armored" personality among elderly persons as being achievement-oriented in a persistent struggle to stay young. The "armored" personality is neurotically striving in an effort to defend against the greatest fear—the fear of growing old. These researchers see the armored personality in a pitiable light. But better to be armored though neurotic than to be disintegrated and despairing. We must not believe that the man or woman who seems "armored" is necessarily neurotic. Work and involvement can be a defense against despair or an offensive thrust toward meaningfulness.

George was the youngest person in the nursing home. Perhaps he shouldn't have been there, really. He was slightly brain damaged, although harmless. His mother who had cared for him all his life had just died, and relatives got his physician to certify him for nursing home care although he had almost no disabilities.

George was very upset with boredom and missing his mother when Ruth met him in a talk group at the nursing home. He quickly moved close to Ruth because she reminded him of his mother. He expressed his boredom and hopelessness at being there "with all these old people." He desperately needed something to occupy his time.

Ruth asked the director to let George sort and deliver mail. George became very proud of his job and was completely able to do it. Now after four years, he is very possessive of his job. He gets up thinking about his important position delivering the mail. Everyone hails him as the "mailman." He constantly asks everyone if they are getting their mail. George will likely be a successful mailman the rest

---

[2] Neugarten, B.L. "Personality and aging." Handbook of the Psychology of Aging. New York. Van Nostrand Reinhold. 1977.

of his life. He gets no pay, and the state inspectors actually frown on the management's possible manipulation of a patient.

But George is happy. He has a reason to live. He loves the old people now and serves them in endless ways. Yes, George is an "armored" compulsive, constant worker. He isn't neurotic, just slightly mentally retarded. But George is immensely happy. He has found his niche. George is a champion.

Neugarten's "integrated personality," in contrast to the "armored personality," is self-assertive while being relatively free from aggressive or defensive feelings and actions. Whether that is better or not, it does describe more reasonably where the majority of maturing champions reside. You are not a champion only if you are healthy, vigorous, and productive. Champions of the eighth span are known by their attitudes.

Is a cancer-ridden person, who smiles his way through intractable pain while he faces each new day with much courage and some joy, a champion? Is the person, who has become more pleasure loving because he simply feels this is the way he wants to live his life, a champion? Of course, they are!

To be fully alive to every opportunity and fully able to make a choice regarding those opportunities, that is the mark of the maturing champion. The choice of what one chooses to do with one's life does not determine a champion. The only true marks of a maturing champion are his values. So long as we place our Christian values and our love of God first in our priorities, we can all be champions!

Chapter 6

LIVING WITH VITALITY

What? know ye not that your body is the temple of the Holy Ghost, which is in you, which ye have of God, and ye are not your own? (I Corinthians 6:19)

We are told on good authority that life expectancy is steadily increasing. While the average life expectancy for Caucasians was 47 in 1900 and 65 in 1950, it has zoomed upward to 76 in the early 90's. Every indication is that it will move even higher.

This is both interesting and important, but of greater import is sustaining your vitality with age. It is not particularly exciting to think about folk living long lives while spending many of the later years in disability, serious decline, and pain. But happily, it may be reported that many people are not only living longer but also with continued vitality. And it is possible for all of us to do so!

Long Life and Short Decline

It is generally thought to be a worthy goal to have folk live long lives of usefulness and meaningfulness, then to decline and die rapidly. In this sense, the ideal would be to have human life take on the qualities of the time-honored One-Hoss-Shay of literary renown. Oliver Wendell Holmes wrote this "logical story" many years ago. The Deacon, according to this story, fashioned for his parson friend a shay which would not last forever but a long, long time indeed. Then instead of "breaking down," it would wear out—disintegrate at a moment in time.

"Fur," said the Deacon, "t's mighty plain
Thut the weakes' place mus' stan' the strain;
'n' the way t' fix it, uz I maintain,
Is only jest
T' make that place uz strong uz the rest."

The one-hoss-shay lasted many years without repair or breakdown because every part was made of equal strength and stamina. But when it went, it went.

What do you think the parson found,
When he got up and stared around?
The poor old chaise in a heap or mound,
As if it had been to the mill and ground.
You see, of course, if you're not a dunce.
How it went to pieces all at once.
All at once, and nothing first,
Just as bubbles do when they burst.

Yes, it is a commendable hope that one day we may have human bodies like that—bodies that are fully functional until they go—all at once. It may come as a surprise to some to know that this aim is at the heart of geriatric medicine. The general aim is that everyone should have long, useful, and unhampered lives ending, since they must end, suddenly or relatively so.

A reasonable goal for all of us is to have lives without torturous disease. Indeed, most <u>infectious</u> diseases have already been conquered. Gerontologists are saying that a disease-free life should end at an average of 85 years. Of course, no one knows what the future will bring; but for researchers, this is the hoped for life expectancy. The number of persons living well past 100 would possibly increase slightly while the number dying before 85 would likely decrease along with a sharp decline in the death rates of young people.

The Human Life Span

Inherent in the prediction of a maximum life expectancy averaging 85 years is the idea that the human life span is fixed by the genetic code. Life span in this context indicates the maximum possible length of life. In reviewing over 600 super-centenarian candidates, it has been found that 116 is the oldest documented age of any person as of 1990. There is a tendency for many quite elderly people to overstate their ages, especially in some cultures.

Every living organism has a genetically-coded maximum life span. Redwood trees at 2000-plus years may represent the longest span, but most authorities agree that 120 years approximates the oldest age to which humans may ever aspire.

Moses, The Prototype

Perhaps Moses should be the prototype for super-centenarians or even people of advanced years. The Bible says, "And Moses was a hundred and twenty years old when he died: His eye was not dim, nor his natural forces abated."(Deuteronomy 34:7) This certainly becomes a goal which we modern humans might well adopt. Obviously, the longevity is much less important than the vitality. Moses died at 120 with "unabated forces." For this reason, along with the many more profound reasons given in the scriptures, Moses' proclamation as the outstanding "prophet" of all times is imminently justified.

Ideal Life, Ideal Death

Yet, for the time, it may be well to think that a life without disease ending on average quite suddenly at about age 85 would be a magnificent achievement and one imminently attainable. Eighty-five years as a maximum average life expectancy was suggested by researchers in 1981[1] when the average life expectancy was 73. By 1990 life expectancy had grown by approximately another three years and likely will keep growing. Researchers have been surprised by the swiftness of the continuous upward spiral of life expectancy. Who knows? Maybe an average age of 90 will turn out to be more realistic.

---

[1] Fries, J.F. and Crapo L.M. Vitality and Aging. W.H. Freeman and Company. San Francisco.

And how do we achieve this longevity and vitality up to age ninety or beyond? To gain some answers, it might be well to look for a moment at the road we have traveled to get to the seventy-six years of life expectancy now extant for Caucasian females.

Historical Perspectives On Infectious Disease

In 1900 there was an extremely high rate of infant mortality. But except for high infant mortality, death occurred almost equally along the life cycle. Obviously, a high rate of infant mortality caused the average life expectancy to remain quite low. Actually, after about 1940 as infant deaths became proportionately fewer, death rates throughout the lifespan remained about the same because of the infectious diseases. Until 1950 or so there was not a sharp increase in life expectancy. However, the death rate caused by the various infectious diseases has changed remarkably in the last forty years. Looking all the way back to 1900, we find that in that year 914 persons per 100,000 population died from tuberculosis. Twenty years later the incidence was down to 154, forty years later down to 46, and seventy years later down to 2 per 100,000 population. Typhoid fever deaths have all but disappeared.

Pneumonia/influenza taken together have been the most persistent with 202 per 100,000 population in 1900 and 31 in 1970. But although diphtheria, whooping cough, measles, smallpox, and other infectious diseases still exist, less than a single person per 100,000 population die from any of these diseases in any single year. So the virtual elimination of most infectious illnesses has raised life expectancy dramatically. Accidental deaths by motor vehicles now cause 27 deaths per 100,000 population each year, the largest single cause of death in the age group under 25 years. Accidents of all kinds represent the largest single cause of death across the entire population.

Disease

so, the focus in medicine was on the infectious
for smallpox came in the 20's, immunizations
30's, for whooping cough and measles in the
under almost total control in the 1950's. New
first the sulfa group, then antibiotics beginning
he killer pneumonia within easy control. No
pidemics and multitudinous others run rampant.
us disease undoubtedly will spring forth just as
scourge in the 1990's, but we have assurance
hat infectious illnesses will kill only the very
ally, Alzheimer's Disease represents a great
ct. No one has discovered what causes it. Some
virus is involved, but even those who do suspect
is not contagious.

perhaps quite rare inasmuch as remaining
ack weak and defenseless bodies, but there is a
hy natural death (death from old-age alone)
on is chronic illnesses.

ersal illnesses have been with us all along, but
the identified killers, these chronic illnesses
der attack early in the twentieth century.
thought of as largely unavoidable and only
e taken with these until the infectious diseases

onic disease usually begins early in life, has a
nature, and emerges in identifiable form
way. For example, atherosclerosis (clogged

arteries) begins in the twenties and plaques with scarring are found in autopsies among the very young who die from accidents. Once these plaques begin to form, they continue and multiply, blocking arteries more and more as life progresses. Many of us simply outlive their serious impact. Others, because of an impeded blood flow, suffer heart attacks, strokes, and other catastrophes or discomforts.

Thus, it is with all the universal or chronic diseases. Unless we control them or delay their impact on our bodies, they kill or render the body weak and vulnerable to remaining infectious microbes. But we can prevent them to a considerable extent, and certainly we can control their progress. With careful body management, we need not die prematurely at seventy-five or at eighty-five from chronic disease. But few will live to die natural deaths from age alone. However, that is the optimal goal—to impede chronic illness until a person can die of old age alone.

Infectious disease is largely conquered, but chronic disease is increasing. Obviously, we should expect chronic disease to increase along with increase in life expectancy.

Among the chronic or universal diseases, some of which will probably invade most of our bodies, are atherosclerosis, arteriosclerosis, cancer, diabetes, emphysema, cirrhosis of the liver, and arthritis. The keys to defeating these as causes of untimely deaths are prevention, early detection, slowing the progression of the disease, and treatment with medication and surgery.

Universal Diseases and Lifestyle

The causes of all chronic diseases is not known, but for some there is a single known cause. For example, cirrhosis of the liver is caused by alcohol consumption and rarely by anything else. Lung and other cancers as well as heart disease are often caused by the nicotine in tobacco. Most chronic diseases have been studied sufficiently so that we know probable causes and risk factors with high degrees of certainty. Some are probably completely unavoidable because they come to us by genetic endowment from family through parents. But even these can usually be detected early and their effects delayed.

Slowing Often Means Preventing

Medical experts strongly suggest that most of us develop cancerous cells and that healthy bodies reject these. If the base cause of getting cancerous cells is genetic, our bodies being sound and virile may continually and constantly reject cancers allowing us full life and natural death. Thus, cancer has been prevented by strong and virile bodies. In other instances, chronic disease is slowed by good health practices. Rheumatoid arthritis may be controlled or slowed by medication. One may have the disease at some level for decades without its contributing to one's natural death. Thus, arthritis is prevented; that is, it is prevented from becoming the killing agent.

These should not be seen as gloomy prognoses. We have once to die, and if this death occurs by natural causes of old age and not by disease, then our destinies will have been fulfilled. We will have our joys, do our work, and go home rejoicing to live with the Lord. But again, we must not confuse long life with optimal life.

The optimal life is more one of vitality than of longevity. There is a happy set of circumstances here. Most chronic illnesses are products of lifestyle. We can know for sure that cirrhosis and many cancers are caused from bad health practices. Most of the chronic illnesses occur as the body fends off insults made to it. Thus, we consistently insult our bodies and organs by working too hard, living with too much stress, smoking, drinking alcohol, using drugs, getting insufficient sleep, etc. The body will retaliate by developing chronic disease.

It is a fortunate circumstance indeed that most if not all the hostile reactions of the body which cause chronic illnesses are reactions to our mistreatment of the body, mistreatments which are not pleasant to begin with. The body does not require that we be joyless, gloomy, and unhappy. Actually, it reacts to insults which are hardly if ever pleasant to the person delivering the insults. In the beginning, smoking is a nauseating experience. It is only as we ignore the body's pleas for kindly treatment that the body reacts with hostility and chronic illness. The body is imminently reasonable.

Your body carries on a dialogue with you that goes something like this: "Be nice to me while enjoying yourself being nice, and I'll be nice to you. Insult me while you also suffer from nausea or drunkenness, and I'll get back at you."

The Body Is the Temple

Most of us abuse our bodies in one way or another. Obviously, this is sinful since our bodies are the dwelling places of the Holy Spirit. When a cherished guest visits us, most of us put our houses in order. We clean the carpets, paint up, and fix up for the visitor.

But the Holy Spirit is not a visitor. The Spirit dwells with us in bodies that often are unkept, unhealthy, and unfit. It would be a labor of love to ourselves to make the best temples possible for our own personal benefits. What then shall we present to the Holy Spirit as a dwelling place? Only the very best it could be!

Keeping Fit Is Mandatory

We who are aging are most fortunate that gifted minds have been moved by God to study the special needs of aging bodies. Gerontology is by definition the study of the "old man." Dedicated physicians are devoting themselves to geriatric medicine as a special calling from God.

We have no choice. We must dedicate ourselves to the preservation of health, stamina, virility, and vitality. Less than total dedication to the fitness principle is an affront to the God who made us.

Some will live with pain, but they must glorify God through the pain. He will call us home in His time. Until He does, we must in the name of fitness study to show ourselves approved. God will accept nothing less than total maximization of our possibilities insofar as keeping fit is concerned, and that means that we must maximize our tripartite selves: our bodies, our minds, and our spirits.

Chapter 7

HOLDING ON, LETTING GO, AND REACHING FORWARD

... but this one thing I do, forgetting those things which are behind, reaching forth unto those things which are before. I press forward toward the mark for the prize of the high calling of God in Christ Jesus. (Philippians 3:12-13)

Have you ever attended a reunion of a class from your high school or college? You were really amazed at how old these people had become! Right? How do you suppose they felt about you?

<u>Are You Growing Old Too?</u>

Most of us do not recognize in ourselves the aging process nearly so sharply as we recognize it in our friends and loved ones. Most aren't really trying to avoid reality. Well, maybe we are reacting to society's dictum that old is bad. Many of us are just too busy to notice the changes in ourselves. Bernard Baruch at age seventy said, "I have always defined old people as those fifteen years older than I am."

Well, that is both good and bad. The good part is that if we don't feel old, we have a tendency to act younger than we really are. We feel good about ourselves. And why shouldn't we? Not feeling old helps us plan for tomorrow and keeps us enjoying the way we are living at the present. We need to feel wonderfully alive, and feeling older helps no one. "You are as old as you feel" is an old truism which isn't exactly true. But I would much rather see you feeling younger than feeling older than you really are. The pluses are mostly on that side of the coin.

So, what's bad about not feeling your age? Well, it does cause some problems for other people. You act the way you feel, and some frictions arise between yourself and others when you don't act the way they think you are supposed to.

Surely, you know some folk, who being elderly, act in ways that deny some of the declining abilities of their bodies. They wind up doing foolish things, expecting older bodies to deliver younger actions. According to some, this makes dangerous drivers out of some elderly folk although statistics largely fail to support these claims. Be cautious; you might actually hurt yourself trying to do something which your bones and muscles are unable to do.

Making Allowances

The point of all this is that as each of us grows older, we must respect our bodies both in their strengths and in their weaknesses. But a more important point is that we do have to release some things, some actions to the realities of change. Change is universal, and you may be understanding me to say that all changes along the highway of life are changes toward decline. Not so at all! So often, we overlook the obvious. Everyone speaks of "growing old." Somehow the word "grow" loses its meaning in the statement.

While change is universal, it is also a central aspect of growth. Without change there is no growth. It is important to know that as a person declines in one thing, he may get stronger in another. We never stop growing although our bodies are in constant decline beginning as early as the mid-twenties. Does that sound like a paradox? Well, it isn't!

Life Is Growth

Modern psychologists consider life a process of growth from cradle to grave. Certainly, this doesn't mean physical growth or even stamina which can be maintained with acceptable change well into the seventies under the best of circumstances. It does mean that one continues to grow in his spirituality, in his understanding of his universe and his place within it, and in his relationship with God.

True, even the full, good life brings us eventually to death, one of the milestones on the road of everlasting life But for the Christian, death is a new beginning.

It could be suggested that our trajectory of travel through our earthly life is like the trajectory of a bullet. It travels until it reaches its destination. As it travels always forward, it loses speed and the trajectory is always downward with the pull of gravity. The analogy is not at all perfect. We humans grow ever forward, but we do so in spurts. While arguably our speed of growth may drop off in some ways as we grow older, there are other ways in which our forward and upward motion unlike the bullet is capricious, coming as it does in spurts of new insights and renewed growth in our relationship both with God and fellow man.

Change and Age

Again, we change as we grow older. Change is one of the few absolutes in this life. Our bodies change, our spirits change, relationships change, and situations change. Time alters our bodies, our attitudes, our insights and our goals. Every phase of life requires some degree of growing up and letting go.

How can we grow and not change, and how can we change without turning loose parts of our lives? Can we stay as children forever? No. As did Paul, we must say, "When I was a child, I spake as a child, I understood as a child, I thought as a child: but when I became a man, I put away childish things." (I Corinthians 13:11) Who would want to stay a child forever either physically, emotionally, or spiritually? But to become an adult, we have to turn loose of childhood although we may permit ourselves from time to time to regress a bit and let the little child within us come out and play.

Somehow, we do not suffer that much in giving up being a child inasmuch as our culture applauds the youth we become when we do give up our childhoods. Most teenagers yearn to be grown ups while being sometimes quite unable to leave comfortable dependency behind. But as one moves along the track of time, giving up things becomes harder. For instance, it is difficult to say goodbye to alma mater and college friends upon graduations. It is difficult for parents to see their young grow up and out. The empty nest syndrome is especially difficult for mothers. But growth demands of all of us that we give up those things that are inherent in a certain stage of life. It is inevitable. We cannot stand still and grow forward!

Are You Fully Grown?

Some early psychologists and psychiatrists charted the life stages of children up to and including adolescence. Thus, Freud postulated the oral, anal, phallic, and genital stages, this last representing adulthood. Piaget did much the same thing charting the cognitive stages of childhood cognition from psychomotor through formal-operations stages. To these psychologists, once a person was grown, he was fully grown and stayed that way forever, or at least until death. More modern psychologists such as Erikson, Maslow, and Rogers recognize that being "grown" is but the beginning of growth toward becoming all that one can become.

As we grow older we become older and growing—growing in spirit and grace, in generosity and caring—at least, that is the way it should be. Yes, growing is painful, for it means losing our grasp on the familiar, the comforting, and the safe. But this is necessary!

The Pain of Growing

As life unfolds, the change and growth become more painful as a rule. A high price in pain is paid in giving the last child to the university, to marriage, and to moving far away. Yes, growing forward exacts a price.

But how much more a price is exacted in refusing to grow! In failing to let go of the past, we can find no meaning in the present and in the enriching experiences of each new day, each new day of our eternal lives.

Some of life's changes are difficult to fit into the "growth concept." The death of a child, a parent, a spouse; the breakup of a marriage; retirement; moving to cheaper, less expansive, and less expensive living quarters—are these not times for tears? Of course they are. So let the tears flow. But ultimately each of us must ask ourselves the question, "Do I try to hang on to that which was, or do I reach out to that which is and might be?"

Bending But Not Breaking

Our capacities to change and to grow will depend on our rootedness. Are we rooted firmly in the promises of God that He will never leave us? Are we rooted in David's declaration, "God is our refuge and strength, our ever present strength in time of trouble"? (Psalm 46:1) As Christians we should be firmly rooted into the ground of our faith. The rigidity of our rootedness should contrast with the flexibility of our confident and flexible stance toward a life that is complex, demanding, and confusing. We Christians stand tall and straight like a flexible tree planted by the rivers of the water of life with roots locked into the rock of ages. We are destined to withstand the storms of stress, frustration, and pain. We can sway with the winds of time and not break. While rigid towers with firm foundations break and collapse, we in our flexibility and rootedness stand firm with the ravages of time. Our strength comes from our constant resistance to stresses. The challenge of change, with its requirements of turning loose those things that are transient, frees us from the past—frees us to examine and determine what we really want, what we really must do with the earthbound segments of our everlasting lives.

77

We must make a friend of change and of challenge; thus, we shall be able to let go of the familiar, the comforting, and the rewarding. We must give our full attention to that which lies ahead. With each new outreach of our lives—the letting go of loved ones who pass, the relationships that did not endure, or the disappointments in people and events—we must give up some cherished illusion of safety so that a larger expansion of our sense of self, of God, and of eternity may come. "Be still and know that I am God . . . He is a rewarder of them that diligently seek him." (Psalm 46:10 and Hebrews 4:6)

Leaning Forward and Reaching Out

As Christians and as human beings, it is necessary for us to lean forward before we reach out. Letting go of things that are no more is not an all or nothing proposition; but in a real sense, we do have to let go of the past in order to reach forward to the future. We must place ourselves in a forward thrusting posture even before we fully know what we are reaching out to embrace. The future for each of us is mysterious, but it will be a puzzlement never solved unless we join with Paul in an attitude of forward movement and forward intent. "...but this one thing I do, forgetting those things which are behind, and reaching forth unto those things which are before, I press toward the mark for the prize of the high calling of God in Christ Jesus." (Philippians 3: 12-13) Thankfully, it is not necessary for us to clearly see the entire road ahead before we may feel free to launch ourselves into the unseen and unknown.

Although many years have passed, the sun still rises and sets, and the world moves on with us or without us. We must reach out to the world and to others regardless of chronological age. The touch of a caring hand at any age is an expression of love. Love unexpressed is love lost. Our capacity for reaching out must be halted only temporarily by our painful losses and the winds of change in our lives. If ours was a serving profession during our active professional lives, we must turn loose of the professional life and reach out to service in new and fresh ways. Never to look back is not a Christian virtue. Never to look forward is certain death for our Christian witness and to our wellness of mind and body.

You Must Make It Happen

We cannot wait for something good to happen. We must planfully make it happen. Our zest for life must not be diminished by circumstance of change or tragedy. We are the creators of our own destinies, our own meanings. Each minute of life can be an unrepeatable miracle that makes the present moment real. Living fully in the present makes the past meaningful and the future possible.

Most of us retire from jobs, vocations, and professions, but we do not nor should we retire our minds. People who do not retire mentally will never grow old at heart.

Never lose your rapacious appetite for what comes next. If you are alive to life, a little voice will tell you, "Never miss a sunrise." As the song says, "And if you should survive to a hundred and five, think of all you'll derive from just being alive. And this is the best part, you'll have a head start, if you are among the very young at heart."

Chapter 8

LIVING PRODUCTIVELY WITH HIGH SELF-ESTEEM

For ye are brought with a price: therefore glorify God in your body, and in your spirit. (I Corinthians 6:20)

In a recent article directed to new parents, Dr. James Dobson, a foremost Christian psychologist, wrote that the greatest gift parents can give their children is a high self-esteem. His reasons for saying this are obvious. If a child does not think positively about himself, he will be unable and unmotivated to live his life with zeal, vigor, and productivity. It is critical for the child, with his emerging personality, to gain high self-esteem.

But isn't having high self-esteem critical for any and all of us at any time of life? It is indeed. We can hardly garner enough courage to do battle with the world in all its complexity if we feel deep inside that we are "no good." It is out of the heart, out of the sense of worth in ourselves as a child of God that righteousness and good works come forth.

Every Person Requires Confirmation

It is essential for a little child to have the feeling of worth which can be given only by his parents as they constantly affirm him both through his being who he is and for what he does. Every single one of us, in order to maintain our sense of purpose in this universe, must possess that gift of self-esteem. At every stage of life we require confirmation from others of our worth, we require approval from God, and very importantly we require approval from ourselves.

Feeling our worth as children of God with a firm belief in our own power to live productively is our way of acknowledging and worshipping the God who made us and who gave us our bodies, minds, and talents for what we are able to do in His service. We must respect ourselves in order to maintain the drive for good works and in order to command respect from others. "To thine own self be true and it follows as night follows day that thou canst not be false to any man." God condemns "foolish pride," but a self-affirmation derived from a sense of one's worth and value as a child of the all-loving God glorifies the God who made us all, who gave us life.

The Aging Suffer Great Losses of Self-Esteem

A child may lose self-esteem because of a single failure for which he gets a harsh and foolish parental reprimand. We who are parents must come to realize how fragile are the egos of some of our children. We can literally crush them with unkind words. Their recovery from well-intended scoldings sometimes takes only a moment, but at other times, the effects last a lifetime. We have learned long ago that some of our children required gentle handling. How fragile is self-esteem! How life-destroying an unkindness can be if it causes the offended to lose faith in himself! Man was made to be only a little lower than the angels, and losing faith in oneself is so shattering as to shake one's faith in God. Self-esteem is the product of the God within us; losing it is like losing God. Finding it again is like finding God again, for self-esteem in a very real sense is the heartbeat of human dignity. "For what is a man profited if he shall gain the whole world and lose his own soul?"(Matthew 16:26) Is not the soul the seat of moral life, and is not self-esteem the linchpin which holds our integrity as persons intact?

The child has a fragile self-esteem. Self-esteem generally grows stronger with age, because in growing up the person finds his sense and source of meaning in his own endeavors. True, a large source of meaning is God Himself, but an important source of meaning in our lives lies in tasks to be done, children to be reared, vocations to be pursued, people to love, and people to love us back. The essence of life is meaning.The presence of God is the source of that meaning but the maintenance of meaning depends on many factors which require the person to reach out confidently into his world. With appropriate self-esteem coupled with appropriate acknowledgement of the source of all gifts, we can make a difference in this world.

As we grow older, it is not as easy to make a difference. With age, self-esteem will dwindle unless the aging person knows how such loss of self-esteem happens, knows what causes it to happen, and knows how to keep it from happening. That is what this chapter is all about—it is about maintaining our self-esteem, our sense of purpose. We must sustain our senses of meaning and of purpose during the aging process. We must not give up the struggle—the struggle to make a difference in the name of and to the glory of God. This chapter centers on the aging process and on maintaining self-esteem right up to the point in time when we join Christ in the heavenly abode.

The World of Competition

It is a harsh and terrible indictment of another to suggest that someone is robbing an aging person of his meaning, of his self-esteem. But this is the world of competition. Not every person who pushes you aside from your meaningful endeavors so that he may enhance his own meaning is vicious. Few are. Most are simply looking for their places in the sun and honestly feel that the older man or woman should move along to make room for them. Surely, the pusher has his own self-esteem to deal with. It should never be the intention of the aging to deny self-esteem to courageous and highly motivated younger people. Young people can save their self-esteem while helping the elderly to maintain their self-esteem just as older people can encourage the young, helping them attain and maintain feelings of worth.

We should not seek self-esteem at the expense of another. However, we elderly people would be ever so foolish if we did not guard the gates to our self-esteem, refusing to allow our meaning in life be stolen away from us. We cannot be so generous, and of course, it isn't generosity at all to feel compelled to move over or along so someone else can have a place in the sun. After all, there is room for all in the world and certainly in the Kingdom of God.

In his old age, David beseeched God to hinder those who sought to hurt him. "Let them be shamed and confounded that seek after my soul. Let them be turned backward and put to confusion, that desire my hurt. . . . Now also when I am old and greyheaded. O God, forsake me not; until I have shewed thy strength unto this generation, and thy power to every one that is to come." (Psalm 70:2: Psalm 71:18)

David identified his enemies as those who "hate me without a cause." The parallel between the present world of unthinking young persons who seem to despise older persons as well as entrepreneurs who seek to take advantage of the elderly is remarkable.

Let Us Not Be Naive

Research has shown that intellectual skills diminish with age beginning usually in the thirties. Other research shows little decline until the sixties depending upon how the research is focused. But don't be misled, any possible decline is so tiny as to be insignificant until and unless serious brain degeneration occurs. It seldom does, although there is an increase in organic brain syndromes (Alzheimer's Disease, for example).

But for the sake of argument, let us say that we aren't quite as bright at sixty as we were at twenty; but neither are we as naive. As a matter of fact, with age and experience, we should be much less naive than we were at an earlier age.

"What are you trying to say?" you may ask. Well, just this: As you grow older you are going to be put down if you are naive enough to permit it. The naiveté comes first of all in not being on the ball enough to know when someone (It doesn't have to be someone younger.) is putting you down. If you know it is happening and just go along with it, maybe you are not just <u>naive</u>, but stupid as well .

Others Rob Away Your Self-Esteem By Their Attitudes

A lot of things can steal away your self-esteem; it often seems that the world of both good and evil forces are out to steal it away. It is not always people who do it; ill health is a vicious attacker of self-esteem. Who can feel worthwhile when they are ill and in pain, not knowing if they will live or die. It could be hoped that your sense of self-worth could weather every storm—storms of illness; of financial loss; of lost loved ones; of loss of jobs, friends, homes, and securities. It is unlikely that you can sail through life without having your sense of worth as a person undermined or even shattered from time to time. The real test is your ability to rebound or to come up from the depths of temporary defeat to reembrace your life of meaning and purpose. "They" may get you down, but "they" can't keep you down!

What Are the Forces That Attack Your Self-Esteem?

Vigilance is the price of liberty and also the price for maintaining self-esteem. You need to know who the attackers of your self-esteem are likely to be. Only by knowing will you be ready to fend off the attackers and to protect yourself. I would like you to know, however, that you can become overly sensitive, and in your sharp awareness you could become skeptical or even paranoid. Not everyone or every force is out to steal your self-esteem; but as you grow older you become more vulnerable to the following: Let me list these, then we'll discuss them at greater length in other chapters.

1. Getting older means giving up roles which have sustained your meanings for thirty of forty years. When you are forced to exit (give up) these roles, you are bound to suffer at least temporary loss of self-esteem. The three main roles which disappear

during the sixth decade of life are work, child rearing, and meaningful relationships. Meaningful marriage relationships can depreciate unless you are vigilant.

2.   Some younger people, in order to promote their lives, will trample on you to make an advance. They may be your fellow workers who want to make you feel old and thus force you out of their way. They may be your children who magnify their youth by imagining that you are old and helpless. If they can make you feel old, then you'll certainly act old. Adult children often attack your self-esteem out of motives not even known to themselves.

3.   Professional people such as physicians, psychiatrists, lawyers, and even ministers see involvement with you as a barrier to their own effective functioning. You are not attractive to them as patients or clients. These people often see you as not worth the time even if you do have more money than anyone else. Some people will take your money and despise you because you took up their time. You may be taken advantage of even by people older than yourself if you seem like a soft touch.

4.   There is a burgeoning market for thousands of items designed to tap the pocketbooks of aging persons. Many of these gadgets have been conjured up by entrepreneurs. These range from special types of toothpaste to special types of condominiums. Unscrupulous home-repair con artists are among the worst of this lot. Never doubt that the entrepreneurs are out to get your money. Even if you can afford to let them have your money, you can't afford to give up your self-respect in the process. Use what they provide, and rejoice with them in your comfort and their profit, but don't be the proverbial sucker. Being a sucker and knowing you are is hard on your self-esteem.

5.   Many people of good intentions get their kicks from helping you. They are the do-gooders, often thinking of themselves as martyrs. They may be your children or close friends. The name of this game is patronization. You must learn the difference between patronization and general kindness. If what they purposely do for you makes you dependent or makes you feel old, then your self-esteem is in jeopardy. As the song says, "People who need people are the luckiest people in the world." But this is true only if you can reciprocate, do something good for them in return. True, one day you will be dependent on others, possibly entirely so. But your self-esteem will remain intact even then if you know you are not being made weaker so that someone else can seem stronger. You can become your own worst enemy if you foolishly decide to sit down in your rocking chair while being perfectly capable of self-management.

You are entitled to enjoy the good life Enjoy it! But don't give up your capacity for self-management when you decide to take it easy. That isn't necessary. Stay on top of the decisions that affect your life—such involvement will add to, not take away from your enjoyment of the good life. Don't believe that taking it easy means you must surrender your own decision-making process. If you decide you no longer desire to be self-managing, you are sure to lose self-esteem although even that is your perfect right .

Chapter 9

YOUR SEXUALITY—TO HAVE AND TO KEEP

Marriage is honorable in all, and the bed undefiled...
(Hebrews 13:4)

Each of us being either male or female have sexuality. We are created as two types of persons, male and female. God, in giving the command to Adam and Eve to be fruitful and multiply, not only approved sexuality but sanctioned sexual behavior in both animals and humans. Sexuality is ours to have, a part of our beings, a very part of ourselves. Sexual behavior is ours to express and to enjoy as a gift. It is approved by God.

Human Sexuality Was Special From the Beginning

God decreed that the fish, animals, and birds as well as man should multiply and replenish the earth. Yet, man and woman stand unique. Sexual behavior for them can be indulged for reasons other than procreation. Sexuality and sexual behavior was bequeathed to humans that each might have pleasure in the body of the beloved. Thus, human sexual desire is a relatively constant drive in both the human male and the human female. This is in stark contrast at least to the female of other species. Female sexual drive for reproduction only is the rule in the female of other mammalian species. God gave Eve to Adam as a helpmeet, one to help meet his needs, one of them being his sexual needs. Correspondingly, God created in Eve a sexual drive that she might not only accomplish that purpose but also fulfill her own purpose, her own needs and her own pleasures.

That Man and Woman Might Know Each Other

Sexuality and sexual behavior were bequeathed to the human person for procreation, for pleasure, for the avoidance of loneliness, and for social and spiritual fellowship and communion between husband and wife.

"And Adam <u>knew</u> Eve his wife; and she conceived." (Genesis 4:1) The biblical description of the sexual act is knowing one another. The expression is fraught with the concept of intimacy, close familiarity, and taking pleasure in the body of the other.

The current generation (especially the younger segment) is often described as having fostered a sexual revolution. Many believe that in this generation we have come at long last to understand the repressive shackles built up over the centuries preventing us from knowing the full joys of sex. This may or may not be true. It is possible that in the beginning husbands and wives had no inhibition about sex and experienced freely the supreme joys even more so than does our liberated generation. We cannot know; but we can be sure that during many generations, moralizing forces did repress sexual freedoms and joys. We are perhaps escaping from these to an extent. It is not yet known whether our relative escape from repressive sex ethics is a blessing and/or a curse or what measure of each may come from the sexual revolution as we are now experiencing it.

Repression Extended Toward the Older Person

We do know that sexual repression for good or for bad was fostered upon the general population in times past and is still with many of us. We further know that those of advancing age are still held under repressive influence more so than is true for younger people. It is plausible that people over fifty are suffering from a double stigmatization insofar as their sex lives are concerned. One stigma arises because people younger than we are not able to understand that we have the capacity and desire to maintain active sexuality. The other is that some of us are still affected by repressive ethics under which we were reared.

Being born fifty or more years ago, both males and females have likely internalized much of the repressive elements of the era of their childhoods. They are victims of an era when sexual behavior was closeted not in bedrooms but in cloistered minds where there was more ignorance than enlightenment. The perpetrators of stigmatized sexuality, although well-meaning in the main, created confusion, prudishness, and a denial of the legitimacy of earnest and honest sharing of bodies as an integral part of a sharing of spiritual gifts between husbands and wives. The scriptural mandate that the two become one certainly has many interpretations. Shall we emphasize the spiritual while denying the physical. Or can we? Or should we?

Is Continuing Sexual Behavior Necessary?

Statistics are readily available to show that there is generally a diminution of sexual behavior with age. Statistics do not reveal whether this slackening is due to physical causes, to lack of interest, or to a subjugation to societal codes of appropriateness. We can be sure that the changes in sexual drive and/or performance come from many causes.

Diminution of sexual behavior should be viewed probably as many-faceted, as inevitable and desirable. Diminution of time spent with one's beloved spouse in intimate relationships is a different issue. Couples should grow closer as the years go by. "Sweeter as the years go by" is a musical refrain intended to describe the relationship between God and man, but it is certainly not inappropriate to apply the sentiment to husband and wife relationships.

The media has it, that with advancing age, there is not less sexual activity certainly not less on the part of males; there is just less within the marriage and more outside. Nothing should be farther from the truth!

Reality? Sexual behavior is much more frequent among married men and women of any age than with their counterparts of spinsters, bachelors, widows, and widowers. And this statement, easily supported by research, is an important reality for young and old married persons.

Married life encourages erotic stimuli. And married life gives far greater promise of release for the stimulated sexual drive. Let us not be misled by the soap opera scenario. There is a strong trend toward making sexual behavior outside marriage attractive. But it certainly should not be that way. Promiscuous sex is sinful on the one hand and destructive to the marriage bond on the other. The lure of promiscuous sex is focused upon Christians by the media. Christian principles, derived from scriptural teaching, should make extra-marital sexual expression disgusting to all Christians. There is, summarily, no need for sexual expression outside the marriage bed. No relationship can escape disagreements which sometimes cause anger and disillusionment. These disagreements must be resolved under divine guidance and not used as excuses for moving outside the marriage for intimacy.

What Are the Possibilities for Sex with Advancing Years?

The best prediction for what will be, is what has been. Uninterrupted continuance of sexual intimacy with one's beloved is found most often among those who have looked upon their sexuality and the expression thereof as something of positive value. Other couples enter into their fifties or sixties with handicaps.

Too often, one or the other of the spouses have various complexes rooted in childhood and continuing into and through the childbearing years. These neuroticisms may cause spouses to approach sexual union with aversion. Sadly, sometimes one spouse is positivistic while the other partner has negative feelings.

Withdrawal From Fulfilling Sex Lives

The male or female spouse who has experienced continuous aversion to sex during early years eagerly seizes upon the excuse of age to withdraw as he/she grows older. Thus, the lessening of sexual desire between spouses may occur and be seen by one or both spouses as something that should have been expected with aging and something that is desirable. Loss of sexual desire with aging is one of the cruel myths of growing old. If either of the partners have embraced this myth, then the sex lives of both spouses will be affected. The results, even for Christians, may be that one of the spouses will seek sexual fulfillment outside the marriage.

The Most Intimate Years

The golden years are ultimately the best for intimacy. There are many reasons why this is true; yet, it will not be true at all unless spouses can deeply know it is true and have no hang-ups that will intervene.

Young spouses beginning their sexual relationships are often frantically driven to emotional excess. In part, this arises because of God's mandate, "Be fruitful and multiply." Urgency is written into God's plan that the world must continue to be populated. More than that, or perhaps as an offshoot of that, young bodies have glandular urgencies which drive them toward love making, joyful union wherein quantity of expression seems more important perhaps than does quality of expression.

Older People, Better Stewards of Time

Relationships are difficult to build and to maintain, and this is becoming increasingly true as the world becomes more complex. With the stresses of modern life wherein each spouse seems driven to enhance self, to make careers productive, and to create personal identities, relationships are often neglected. Because personalities of husband and wife are often so different, and in part because of modern emphasis on the equality principle of husband and wife, stress marks and serious cracks unerringly appear in many marriage relationships. Hence, the horrendous divorce rates result. Recent research reveals that spouses at age sixty are experiencing divorce at about the same rate as applies to the population across the board.

Ken Dychtwald[1], author of <u>Age Wave</u> with Joe Flower and a practicing group counselor for the aging, reports the following case: A seventy-eight year old woman divorced an eighty-one year old husband on being made aware of her extended life expectancy. She said she didn't want to be married to "that jerk" any longer.

Dychtwald and Flower speculate that women as opposed to men will likely experience more logical reasons to end a bad marriage after fifty years or so because the woman has a much longer remaining life expectancy. Upon realizing that they have a promise of more than twenty years of remaining lives, both men and women may, with these insights gained through new knowledge, decide not to remain in unhappy relationships.

But marriages do survive; and, as husband and wife reach advanced years together, the rule seems to be that their commitments to each other too often take on a flavor of "sticking it out because there is no other choice."

What a sad reality, that spouses in their later years sometimes seem more enemies than friends. Few marriages can expect to be so smooth that no hurtful conflicts will arise. What a shame that spouses cannot always forgive and forget, leaving old wounds completely healed and forgotten.

---

[1] Dychtwald, Ken and Flower, Joe. <u>Age Wave</u>. Jeremy P. Tarcher, Inc. Los Angeles. 1989.

Jim and Susan Black lived quite happily through the first five years of marriage and the birth and growth of two beautiful children. Then Harry was born. Harry was an awkward, troubled child from the beginning. Although not mentally retarded, neither was he as bright as were his siblings. Jim had trouble accepting Harry because his ego was too big to admit that he had fathered a child who fell far short of his hopes.

The details are unimportant. The results are dramatically sad. Jim and Susan who were bound together by relative catastrophe instead of by mutual love, respect, and admiration drifted apart. They became spiteful toward each other. Each had affairs during the most tumultuous times of Harry's growing up.

But now Harry has found his personal peace. He has completed high school against heavy odds, has found a good productive job, and has married a lovely girl. Jim and Susan are proud grandparents to Harry's little boy; and Harry himself has grown into mature manhood with more love and devotion to his own parents than that shown by the other two siblings, both of whom are into affluence. These two are prideful and not very supportive of their aging parents. Not so with Harry and his wife, both of whom adore Jim and Susan.

But Jim and Susan live in a bickering turmoil because of hurts inflicted upon one another during the hectic years when Harry was such a problem. They cannot forgive each other, although deep in their hearts they are lonely for each other and desperately need each other.

Variations of this theme are played out endlessly among older couples. Of course, it is summarily foolish. If there is no forgiveness, one will be looking into the casket of the other in a few years. Maybe then for the remaining one, the rancor will ease.

The Games that Spouses Play

Adult children who are alert enough to notice, often marvel at the manners in which elderly fathers and mothers rip each other apart with malicious and usually unconscious "games." Eric Berne in his book Games that People Play[2] describes games as transactions between two people in which one or both have hidden agendas comprising ulterior motives which severely frustrate and damage the person who is the "goat" of the game. A wife may scold her husband for being late for dinner, knowing that he cannot help being late. The husband, under the goad of her tongue lashings, may start being later than necessary. This causes still more severe railing which causes still more tardiness. This example of double gamesmanship could be observed with hundreds of different twists, and the spouses may keep it up for years, not fully knowing what they are doing to one another.

If a marriage counselor had opportunity to work with such people as the above, the two could be persuaded to talk one to the other in the presence of the counselor and under the umbrella of God's love. The counselor's presence would create a sobering effect which could be counted upon to keep tempers under control; and hopefully, each spouse would come to understand the foolish games he/she is playing. With proper help through counsel, prayer, and love for each other, the two may become much happier in the relationship.

Husbands and Wives Should Rally to Support Each Other

It would seem to be common and almost mandatory that husbands and wives quickly rally to support one another when meanings are threatened, but such is not often the case. Husbands do not always, perhaps not even usually, understand the wives' problems *vis à vis* menopause, for example. Neither are they routinely and

---

[2] Berne, Eric. Games That People Play. Grove Press. New York. 1964.

appropriately concerned about the empty nest syndrome since this syndrome brings disproportionate stress upon the mother. Most men are still very involved at this point with work roles.

Unfortunately, marital infidelities during the later years, while not the rule, are not at all rare. This is true for both husbands and wives. Indeed, marriage counselors are needed in the later years far beyond their use. Many elderly couples do not have the motives for correcting problems this late in life, and problems are too often left to fester and worsen therewith exacerbating every problem of alienation and withdrawal already discussed.

Elderly spouses should be especially supportive each to the other, and they certainly can be. Just how to bring about the sensitivities needed to encourage this mutual help is a puzzling proposition. Husbands are in a perfect position to be maximally helpful to wives with lost meaning, and certainly the opposite is true! It is also true that many spouses do help, but not to the extent they could and should. This represents a rich opportunity for an educational ministry with the elderly within the framework of planned church programming.

The power of God ministered through the Body of Christ offers the best available hopes for making the elderly spouses sensitive to the needs of each other. Christ and His love are sufficient for all needs, but His will and His love often depend upon human instrumentation.

Leave the Past Behind

The rule is and should be that youngsters grow up, engage their own lives, and have increasingly less time for aging parents. This is as it must be and should be. With the aging parents moving on into their own futures, the spouses need each other as never before.

Please allow this writing to help you, the aging spouse to find the beauty, the dearness, and the integrity of your spouse. It can be accomplished through the spirit of love; which begins in the love of God for His creatures, moving to the love of human creatures for God, and eventuating in the love of man for woman, spouse for spouse. Give up blaming, carping, demeaning, humiliating, and belittling your spouse. Rekindle the wounded spirit of love and allow God to heal the wounds.

Return to Intimacy

Aging people must learn more about intimacy. In the younger days, most confused intimacy with sexual need. Indeed, sex was created that the two might become one in body and one in a spirit of communion. Sex should never have been just a physical act, although we may forgive ourselves if it once was that; we cannot allow that misguided notion to continue into the golden years.

Sexual intercourse should be the ultimate in intimacy, but it certainly is not intimacy itself! While disclaiming sex as a necessary aspect of intimacy, we must not fail to recognize the importance of sex as an asset to intimacy as we pass the milestones of the fiftieth, sixtieth, seventieth, eightieth, or ninetieth years. What a beautiful thing old love (yes, including the sexual) is between spouses who have forgiven themselves and each other for personality flaws and transgressions against the bodies and spirits of each other.

Sweeter As the Years Go By

Yes, Jesus' love grows sweeter as the years go by. And so should conjugal love! It is happening every day. But it doesn't happen happenstance.

It is worth the effort of work, of devotion, of forgiveness, of adaptation. It is worth dedication, hard work, and sleepless nights. It is worth maintaining even in the face of abuse, which is sometimes inevitable as the health and stability of one or both spouses crumble in the late, late years.

Make the Most of the Best

Knowing as we must that the failing bodies of spouses will likely yield adverse circumstances as the end of life approaches, we must make the absolute best of the good years together while maturing reigns supreme and infirmity is held at bay. And with the help of God, the new longevity, which is of God and of our own informed perseverance, intimacy may last thirty or forty years beyond the time many couples call it quits. After all, our children have flown the nest, so our energies and thoughts may return to loving each other. Most of us can expect to enjoy thirty to forty years of happy living and loving.

The Best of Sexual Intimacy

It is said that all good things come to him who waits. Well, waiting is not that much a virtue; but having perhaps waited, we cannot blame anyone but ourselves if we fail to enjoy the best. And sexual intimacy in the golden years can be the best! Again, not that sexual intercourse is the end, but it does comprise a large measure of the means to attain a blissful oneness with one's spouse.

Just as God decreed that the human species should enjoy sex almost on a constant basis as contrasted to other life forms, He has decreed that this glorifying act of oneness and communion could be enjoyed into very advanced years. The brain is the most important sex organ, and the brain, to a large extent, can control human genitalia. The critical elements are attitude and expectation.

Sexual Behavior Does Not Require Going All the Way

During our pre-fifties, most of us felt a strong sense of frustration if on initiating a sexual encounter, we were unable to release the tension via orgasm. Orgasm may continue to be possible for both male and female even into the nineties. But as the golden years come, orgasm should not become a goal which spells virility of either man or woman.

For the male, sexual performance has been the hallmark of manly virility. Obviously, more is required of the male even if we lay aside the active-passive context of male versus female sexual intercourse. Actually, many studies have been made showing women to be more orgiastic than men. But these research findings are of little importance in this discussion.

It Is the Closeness that Counts

Throughout the advancing years, qualitative and quantitative differences come into the sex act. Sexual intercourse per se between older spouses becomes less frequent. That is no catastrophe. The orgiastic nature of sexual release (if any) will change with the years. That is no catastrophe either. Male erection and ejaculation will take on quantitative and qualitative differences. No catastrophe! Female orgasm will be different if indeed it occurs at all. Still, no catastrophe.

The catastrophe is that many elderly couples do not choose to press their bodies together in loving embraces. That elderly spouses cease and desist from embracing, lying together, caressing, offering pleasant tactile stimulation one to the other, is indeed a sad neglect. True, many have denied these needs for so long that there may no longer be a felt need. What a pity!

The human spirit at any age reaches out to God. Likely this is more true as people age. Except for foolish societal codes embedded in concepts of sex as inappropriate for the aging, older bodies and spirits would have more of a need for closeness as the years unfold. With the denial of sex as a need for older persons has come a denial for any intimacy at all. It is a catastrophe that some people do not know or appreciate this. Touching is for everyone. The very special touching which develops sexual stirrings is properly reserved for the special relationships of conjugal sharing in marriage.

There is nothing that can take the place of the human touch. Older bodies, most of all, yearn for the human touch. True, some have denied this for so many years that they may develop a tendency to shrink from the touch of hands. But this has occurred because of gross errors perpetuated over years of self-denial and lack of feeling and knowledge.

Human bodies never become so wrinkled, so shrunken, or so physically debilitated that they do not deserve to be touched. Again, this statement presupposes that a human most often desires the touch and caress of a fellow human of their own approximate age group. Denials of this principle are on every hand as older women desire much younger men and older men desire much younger women. But these phenomena must be seen for what they are. They are evidences of sickened minds and spirits which have yielded to faulty learnings promoted in unstable childhoods and environments. On the other hand, such unusual intimacies are the result of a society which discourages continued intimacy between spouses into the late years.

Some Logical Qualifications

A recent no-sex poll made by Ann Landers brought a response from 35,000 people. According to these responses, sixty-five percent of couples over sixty-five years of age reported that they no longer engage in sex or do so infrequently. Seventy-five percent of those over seventy responded in like fashion. People who are negative toward sex are more likely to respond to a poll like this, so this cannot be reasonably thought of as scientific research.

However, it is interesting to note that those whose letters were printed, revealed little sex but a lot of cuddling. And that is the real point. Sex can be defined in many ways, and arguably one might say that cuddling is a sexual expression.

Sexual climax becomes less important to elderly people than does other forms of intimate playfulness. It is likely that many couples cease full sexual involvement before they need to. Maybe they cease before they should for health's sake. Many physicians believe that continuation of sex to orgasm, even if infrequent, yields health benefits via beneficial hormonal stimulation.

Elderly couples who engage in touching, caressing, and cuddling should not feel reticence about proceeding to orgasm. However, special knowledge should accompany sexual intercourse in the later years. The following points are important:

1. As women age, the vaginal membranes become thinner and lubrication is less adequate. Too much friction can be uncomfortable and sometimes damaging.

2. Males cannot sustain erections for prolonged periods when they are older. At the same time, more stimulation is necessary for completion of the sex act.

3. There may be vast differences in the sexual appetites of husband and wife. Neither should impose himself or herself to the discomfort of the other. Each should, however, make special efforts to be accommodating, adapting to the needs of the other. Honest and earnest sharing of feelings becomes a must.

4.   Many efforts at coital sex for older people will result in failure for both spouses if orgasm is counted as success. There is, summarily, no reason why orgasm should be recognized as the only measure of success. Pleasure without discomfort to either should be the measure of success.

Each spouse needs the affirmation of the other in the act of one giving pleasure to the other. As long as mutual caring and affirmation of worth toward the other occurs, any intimate contact may be referred to as sex and most importantly as successful sexual performance. On the other hand, there is no mandate that such sharing should be called sex or sexual. The loving caress is sexual if it causes sexual response. If it doesn't, it is still an act of love.

Chapter 10

SOCIAL LIVING THROUGH FELLOWSHIP

"This is my commandment that you love one another, as I have loved you." (John 15:12)

What happens to people's social lives as they grow older? There is little doubt that many persons begin a gradual retreat from social contact, and that social withdrawal begins for most people when the children are gone and the tendency to withdraw gets more pronounced as either man or woman leaves his/her job.

Is it a good idea for aging persons to withdraw from the stresses of work and busy social lives in order that their tired bodies may remain healthy and strong? My quick answer to that question is a resounding "no"!

However, Cumming and Henry (1961)[1] wrote that "disengagement is normal during the aging process." This seemingly dramatic announcement came more than a quarter century after the enactment of Social Security legislation which identified 65 as the point of having gained the privilege of not working anymore. Disengagement theory, seen at its inception as a boon to the aging, began to rear its ugly head about 1935. Social Security legislation, which grew out of disengagement theory, has often been seen as politically motivated. Social Security legislation, for good or for bad, has made it possible for aging persons to withdraw or retreat from work. An unexpected fact is that they have often at the same time have withdrawn from responsibility and from active life. All this ostensibly took place in order to permit the aging persons to preserve their waning strength.

Disengagement would make it possible for older people to look forward to longer and healthier lives, or at least disengagement theory

---

[1] Cumming, E. and Henry, W.E. Growing Old. Basic Book. New York. 1961.

said it would. Sociology, psychology, and gerontology have largely debunked disengagement theory. Countless studies have shown than disengaging from work, from social roles, and from physical activity, brings decadence, disease, and untimely deaths. The activity theory has replaced the disengagement theory, and now countless studies are showing that people live longer, happier, and healthier lives with continued activity within limits.

Social Disengagement Is the Emphasis

As a theory, disengagement turned out to be ridiculous. But then, disengagement from life has always been a reality for aging people whether or not someone developed a theory about it. It is difficult to say which form of withdrawal comes first as a person ages. Some say disengagement likely begins when the breadwinner (usually the husband) leaves the work force. But usually, prior to this event, in the lives of typical couples, the parenting role has already been left behind.The nest is empty, and unavoidably, some social activity is lost when the children depart. But even with an empty nest, socialization continues in families who are in the work force. The ripple effects that comes from employment reach out to engage couples and families with other couples and families ad infinitum. Bonds of friendship, as a rule, are maintained better between people who view each other as equals and who have common interests and experiences to share. But with these companionships receding as they do when people give up work and parenting roles, socialization opportunities decline. Aging couples stay home more and more—it just doesn't seem worthwhile to go to the effort to socialize.

Socializing with Children, In-Laws, Grandchildren

Many aging persons derive tremendous benefits from socializing with their children and their families. When this really occurs, it is wonderful; but in the main, generational differences are too great to permit families to fill the void that comes from withdrawing from people one's own age. The children (now grown and with families) typically have social resources that go along with their own work and parenting roles. They often concede to social relating with their elders with some degree of disdain and discomfort. Many children see keeping in touch with parents as an expected but unwanted chore although most of them do conform to societal expectations. Actually, the young grandchildren often become closer to grandpa and grandma than the children.

It is an open question whether or not having children nearby at one's beck and call is a social advantage. Certainly, there are pluses and minuses. To say the least, aging persons need opportunities to meet and associate with members of their own generation, and as said before, family relationships will not fill the entire social needs of elderly people.

In terms of morale among older persons, several studies have shown that older persons, who see their children often, do not have as high morale as those who see them less. It is often true that children bring with them a host of their own problems when they visit, and the older persons suffer worry and frustration from sharing in these family troubles. This is such a mixed and confusing area of thought that no solid conclusions can be drawn, but is seems safe to say that satisfying family relationships are more likely to exist when the older persons have their own independent social resources and are not compelled to depend on family for social outlets. People who have all their social contacts within the family suffer dependency in both directions. Parents often pay a high price for family social relationships. The price is often financial and too often involves child care which can become onerous to many aging persons.

Enter the Forces of Christianity

Christian fellowship is becoming more important as the complexities of the social, economic, and occupational worlds expand.

Obviously, there was never a time when such fellowship was not important, even crucial. Early Christians could never have survived had they not drawn the bonds of love and fellowship around themselves. The early Christians were fighting enemies about which we know virtually nothing. They were persecuted for their belief in God and Jesus Christ, and within the bonds of His love they found love and fellowship in each other. The local churches became avenues of support through which early Christians found joy in each other, embracing each other in fellowship, a fellowship derived from God through Christ. "That which we have seen and heard declare we unto you, that ye may have fellowship with us and truly our fellowship is with the Father, and with his Son Jesus Christ." (I John 1:3)

Is It Better Today, Or Even Worse?

Fellowship of Christians with each other usually encouraged by church attendance has continued to be a thing of beauty and necessity. There are critics of the organized church and of Christianity in general who profess amazement, demonstrating a total lack of understanding that in our complex world, churches and Christianity not only survive but are growing and expanding. Critics shake their heads in disbelief. "How could this be? Why don't the forces of Christianity crumble?" Indeed, the enemies though different from those of the early church, are more tenacious. The tools of Satan for the demolition of the forces of Christ are sharp and subtle, but still the churches and Christianity survive.

The church has become a haven for young and old, for people of every walk of life. People are flocking with great zeal to their churches, seeking a fellowship that cannot be found in country clubs, discos, gambling casinos, and social ventures developed ad infinitum by modern entrepreneurs. You cannot obtain this type fellowship anywhere except in the fellowship growing out of the bonds of love for Christ and for one another! In part, the renewal of churches everywhere can be credited to the desires of godly folk who seek companionship, fellowship, and social contact which does not follow the familiar worldly patterns of sex, violence, use of drugs, and a general flaunting of the laws of God. The worldly community has changed, has fallen short of providing wholesome social outlets.

Aging in the Religious Community

All that has been said above applies to young and old. Still, the young in school and in college have attractive outlets for social energies. Young married people and parents have outlets associated with their parental, vocational, and success-oriented endeavors of business mixed with pleasure. There is inherently nothing wrong with social life outside the church. True, these social contacts do not usually involve fellowship in and through the Lord. While Christian fellowship is irreplaceable, it is not the only wholesome and meritorious style of social relations.

But again, most of these social outlets crumble with aging. Couples may maintain good social outlets through a variety of secular activities deriving from various club activities. Communities of older people are springing up under entrepreneurial management, and these deserve praise in terms of providing social amenities. The American Association of Retired Persons is doing much in conjunction with government-funded programs to provide social contacts and outlets.

It is true, though regrettable, that many aging persons have no histories of church relatedness. Indeed, many older people find church relatedness for the first time because of the outreach of the church. This is a fine opportunity for churches to extend their outreach program.

It is likely that the lack of social contact and the negative effects of loneliness are more damaging and traumatic to those who have lost spouses and find themselves virtually alone. The Bible is sharply and unwaveringly succinct in instructing the disciples of the Lord to care for the widows and orphans. The outreach programs of churches are doing much, yet not enough to bring Christian fellowship to all who through the aging process find themselves alienated from the mainstream of life.

The Church Has Endless Opportunities

Far from becoming the point of last resort for aging folk seeking fellowship, companionship, and social outlets; the church if it is functioning according to New Testament commandments and imperatives, will become the first resort for all Christians as well as those who can through such ministry be won to a saving relationship with Christ. It is a mistake to think of the family of God as excluding anyone. We cannot by our own judgment exclude anyone from the family of God.

However, every congregation of baptized believers has the right to feel a special fellowship in Christ toward one another. Sadly, some churches have tended to become exclusive, in subtle ways issuing invitations only to those who fit prescribed criteria such as race, social class, level of income, etc. Christ has said that "whosoever will" may come and take of the waters of life freely. Surely, this invitation includes an invitation to fellowship on a social level.

One Body, Many Bodies

One appropriate interpretation is that the Church is the Body of Christ and there is only one Body of Christ. However, in speaking of New Testament churches, it is clear that the majority of references to "the church" is that of a group of baptized believers, who teach, preach, and promote the kingdom from within a local body of believers.

Reaching Out and Moving In

Yes, it is appropriate that churches reach out with a social ministry to persons at every stage of life. This may consist of Vacation Bible Schools, of sports centers on church property, fellowship halls where meals are served, and celebrations of life and of the Lord ad infinitum.

It is certainly appropriate that the church should provide space, leadership, and a strong invitation to those who are growing older. This need is prevalent and should become a part of the thinking of active-minded church leaders. This appropriately may be called outreach although a concerted outreach must touch lives at many points, especially the lives of those who cannot participate in planned activity programs scheduled on church premises. Outreach must touch the lives of house-bound, nursing-home-bound, and hospitalized persons to mention only a few.

Yes, the church has these "callings" which are in every way scriptural although certainly tailored to modern dilemmas. But those elderly who feel abandoned, insecure, and alienated within the social realm should not wait for invitations, coercions, or pleadings.

In every sense of the word, you are a person of choice. If you suffer social alienation, don't wait for someone to reach out to you. Your "calling" is to move into a fellowship which is there waiting for you.

Many if not most of you know very well that the church fellowship is there waiting in the same sense that the Savior waited for you to open the door to your own eternal life. You must appropriate for yourself the courage to act. Return to your church if you have left it; become again a part of the Body of Christ.

It is often true that many of us grudgingly await the pleas and pressures of active church members. We are all perfectly capable of feeling that we have been rejected and that someone from the church has a duty to make a strong and concerted effort to coerce us back into the fellowship. We humans are amazing creatures; we often wait for others to do what only we can do while the days and years slip by. Yes, it takes courage, and especially so, if you are basically a shy person. As life treats some of us rather harshly, it is only natural that we develop some self-pity and with it a reluctance to do for ourselves what we know would be very rewarding to ourselves. We wallow in the morass of our long-term hurts, our bruised egos often derived from some single incident of the past in which we may justifiably feel that we were sinned against. If you were sinned against at one time, that sinner must deal with his own actions. Your question put directly to yourself must be, "Am I sinning against myself with my unforgiving attitudes? Am I holding onto old grievances for all the wrong reasons?"

If you are living a joyless life, it can be joyous again. You can return to fellowship—a fellowship with the perfect Christ and a fellowship with imperfect followers of Christ.

Chapter 11

KEEPING YOUR MIND SHARP

And Moses was a hundred and twenty years
old when he died. His eye was not dim,
nor his natural forces abated. (Deuteronomy 34:7)

Do you think as fast and as sharply as you did when you were twenty? Most folk over fifty would say, "No, of course not." And that is really sad, because most of these folk could be thinking just about as well as they ever did. It is a myth that getting older automatically makes you slow down intellectually. But the myth is winning. That's terrible, isn't it?

I must absolutely insist that, as the song says, "It ain't necessarily so." I must convince you that if you think you are losing your brain power, then you <u>will lose it</u> to a frightening extent! As the Bible says, "For as he thinketh in his heart, so <u>is</u> he." (Proverbs 23:7) You simply can't maintain your sharpness when you yourself are convinced you are losing your brain power.

<u>Intellectual Decline with Age: Myth and Reality</u>

There is a great deal of debate over how aging affects the human brain. Some are saying that the human brain, especially in thinking and reasoning, changes very little in the average person. Indeed, this is what recent research is finding. All of us would probably be pleased to think that our brain power remains the same as we get older. That would be comforting, I guess; but it's not altogether true. But the truth does sound pretty good, even so.

I am going to be talking to you in this chapter about the latest research on the human brain and the way it works in thinking and in reasoning. I can tell you that research being performed by psychologists, neuroscientists, and gerontologists is throwing a lot of doubt on earlier ideas that when you get past middle age, your brain power goes away. Gerontologists are a new breed of scientists who are dedicated to studying "the old man." You are already familiar with geriatric medicine, which is devoted to medical treatment of the elderly. The new breed of scientists are not always right in what they find out; but they are probably a lot closer to the truth than earlier researchers who had a doomsday outlook about growing older.

None of us should expect to be like Moses. God allowed Moses to live 120 years without any decline in any part of his body. We can't do that. Growing old is bound to change our bodies. We must expect that. Expecting changes, we will learn how to live with changes. Actually, we've been doing that ever since we were born. Right? We weren't the same at twenty-eight as we were at eighteen or at eight years of age. But change is not usually bad and there is no reason for us to think that the changes taking place in our bodies in late life are all bad. Maybe some are, but some may be good. Mostly, it depends on our attitudes.

Of course the human brain changes with age, but it changes a lot more between age eight and eighteen than it does between forty-eight and sixty-eight. And both those changes can be good, especially if you are expecting them to be good. Most modern research is emphasizing that the physical brain changes little (in its functioning capacity) from middle age to about age seventy-five. And modern research is showing that our thinking and reasoning power does not change very much during that time either. The trouble is, most of us have been brainwashed to believe we will fade out in our thinking and reasoning powers after fifty or so. This is the myth we mentioned earlier that has been created by bad research and by a lot of forces around us that would like for us to think we are fading in brain power as we get older.

Now again, I don't want you to try to be another Moses who didn't lose anything with age. I do want you to think with me about how the myth of aging is making us non-productive long before we need to be. And I will tell you in this chapter about the research that shows how absolutely wrong the myth of fast-fading intellectual ability is. I will show you how our own attitudes become the real key as to whether we must take a back seat, thinking that getting older makes us less capable of thinking clearly.

Don't Put Yourself Down

Many of us are putting ourselves down and doing a lot of self-pitying. As I said, I am not saying that our intelligence doesn't change with age at all; nevertheless, I do want to see us use all the intelligence we have, to make the best use of what we have, and not to listen to things that don't apply to us. We are too smart to let a myth control our lives.

The Truth Is:

All I have said above assumes, of course, that we have not had a stroke or some physical condition that really <u>does</u> affect our brains. Sure, I know some of you have had problems. But God gave you a strong gift of intelligence. He didn't give us all the same amount to start with—we know that. And even if you are among the unfortunate ones who have had strokes and the like, and if because of this you are not as sharp as you used to be, He expects you to use what you have to the maximum.

No, He didn't start each of us out alike in intellectual gifts and what's more, we are all undergoing changes. We are not changing alike either. It makes no difference. Most of us have a far greater gift of intellect than we have ever used. As we get older, it just may be necessary for us to use a little more of what we've got. So, if you are on a "self-pity kick" because you've heard that older people often lose the use of their minds, that way of thinking has to change. Is such self-pity a way of sinning against God? Well, you be the judge. Most of us are smarter than we think although some are also stupidly denying it for one reason or another.

Intellect or Wisdom?

I have been studying people professionally for over forty years, and I think I have heard it all. I remember the time when psychologists were patronizing older people by saying, "Well, your brain doesn't work as well as it used to; but not to worry—your age has given you wisdom which is far more important than the smart-alecky brain power of the young."

Well, the wisdom part is certainly right. We have learned to use our gifts wisely, to discover how to make things happen with less physical power and less mental strain. I'll buy that. Proverbs certainly agrees. "Wisdom is the principal thing . . . ," Solomon said.

About two years ago, I was working to clear a piece of land. I was in the woods with a young man half my age, and I challenged him that I could cut down an eight-inch sapling faster than he could. I had my tree on the ground with about a dozen strokes of the ax. He, with his young strength, whittled at his tree for a quarter of an hour; and when he finally got it down, the stump looked like a beaver had chewed it down. Did I gloat? You bet I did, but I shouldn't have.

You see, I had the wisdom, and he had the strength. (Actually, I had the wisdom and the strength. Ha!) Although this was a physical contest, you can see how mental situations might take on the same pattern. Wisdom is gained by experience, and wisdom wins at least a lot of times over both physical strength and pure intellectual power.

How Important Is Intellectual Power?

I think you will agree when I say that our society almost worships intellectual power. Every parent is constantly anxious about whether or not their children have high I.Q.'s (intelligence quotients). Teachers always look at the child's record to see what he made on an intelligence test, how smart he is, and how quick he is to catch on. Even people our age are really concerned about our supposedly declining I.Q.'s.

For the moment, let's consider intelligence to be what Solomon was talking about in Proverbs. We'll have some trouble with this, because there are some ways in which intelligence as understood by teachers and wisdom as understood in Proverbs are not quite the same. Of course, God knows all about these little differences in the meanings of words, and we probably never will—not fully anyway.

Be that as it may, Proverbs shows that our modern society is not the only society that was so concerned about wisdom and intelligence. No, not at all. Listen to what Solomon has to say about wisdom, and we'll consider a little later whether or not he meant the same thing or a different thing from what our world is calling intelligence. "Get wisdom, get understanding; forget it not; neither decline from the words of my mouth. Forsake her not and she shall preserve thee; love her, and she shall keep thee." (Proverbs 4: 5, 6). "For wisdom is better than rubies; and all the things that may be desired are not to be compared to it." (Proverbs 8: 11).

So wisdom has always been a very important thing in a happy and fulfilled life. Maybe we have come to place too much emphasis on intelligence and I.Q. scores, but on wisdom—never. For you see, "The fear of the Lord is the beginning of understanding . . . ." (Proverbs 1: 7). "The fear of the Lord is the beginning of wisdom . . . ." (Proverbs 9: 10).

From all this, we must understand that wisdom is something you get, and you get it from the beginning by knowing who the Lord is and by giving Him the Lordship over your life. Only then can you move forward to get other wisdom and other understanding. But again, wisdom and understanding comes from your efforts in "getting." Keeping your wisdom and knowledge will come from your efforts to keep them as much as you possibly can against all odds. You will, or course, give them up to some extent before God calls you home. Before you die, within the providence of God, you may have to give up some wisdom and knowledge as your body fails—as it pleases God. But don't give them up either because of laziness or because someone tells you that you should give these up because you are growing old. You must ignore the voices of the world and continue to grow in wisdom and knowledge.

Again, intellectual power ultimately changes with age—that's God's plan. Time is in His hands and He'll allow things to happen to you in His time, not yours. Don't take God's time into your own hands and suffer an untimely let down of intellectual power.

Changing Bodies and Changing Brains

Outdated research and human error have joined together to suggest that intellectual power must decline because of physical aging. The fact is that nobody has yet proved that intellectual power actually declines with age, with or without the hand of God, certainly not to the same degree that physical strength most often does decline. It is clear that while the brain is part of our physical bodies, that particular part of our physical selves changes at a much slower rate (functionally) than the rest of our bodies.

Fluid Versus Crystallized Intelligence

Until the last ten years, researchers used the word intelligence to indicate what we mean when we say, "That child is really bright." Brightness was thought to indicate that a child (or any person, however old) "caught on" to new and novel ideas easily and quickly. Thus, intelligence in the early years of psychology and gerontology was thought of as a measure of a capacity to learn and to learn quickly. Almost all the thousands now attending college were tested for intelligence with I.Q. tests that were constructed so as to measure their capacity for learning and their quickness to grasp new information. Thus, intelligence was both capacity to learn and an agility in learning.

People who are older do lose some of the quickness, agility, and flexibility younger bodies naturally have. Researchers reasoned that the "muscles in the brains of older folk" lost agility and flexibility just as the muscles of the body did. And knowing they were trying to measure agility and quickness, the researchers made their I.Q. tests to measure just that. And, of course, since the tests did measure capacity to learn, quickness, and agility, older persons who took these tests showed a rather sharp decline beginning at about age thirty-five. This view of intelligence had nothing to do with the amount of knowledge a person might have had. A person might be totally ignorant and still have high intelligence; that is, he might be able to catch on to new ideas quickly and easily. On the other hand, a person might be very knowledgeable but not highly intelligent. He may have worked hard enough in spite of his lower intelligence so as to gain a lot of information.

Let's Get the Whole Story

So long as intelligence was defined as "being quick and bright," and so long as the I.Q. tests were made to measure just that and not made to measure knowledge and understanding, it was hard for Bible scholars to find scriptures relating to intelligence. As far as I have been able to determine, the word "intelligence" is not in the Bible.

Anyway, about ten years ago, gerontologists started thinking about a different kind of intelligence. The older idea of intelligence, being brightness, was labeled fluid intelligence. The new definition of intelligence now being used in research is called crystallized intelligence and is defined as "a usable and useful fund of knowledge

119

together with attendant skills in using such knowledge." Thus, the new concept of intelligence is a measure of how much knowledge we have and how well we use that information. This is certainly not the same as the older concept of <u>fluid</u> intelligence (intelligence that figuratively jumps over fences, is agile, and highly flexible).

So psychologists are making new tests designed to measure this new concept of intelligence. And what do you know? This research put a much different light on it. Using a new way of testing which was designed to measure <u>crystallized</u> intelligence, researchers found very little decline in I.Q. until about age 60[1]. Many people showed no decline until age 74.

Schaie says:

At the risk of possible overgeneralization, it is my general conclusion that reliably replicable age changes in psychometric abilities of more than trivial magnitude cannot be demonstrated prior to age 60, but that reliable decrement can be shown to have occurred for all abilities by age 74. (Schaie, 1983b, p. 127)

By age 74, almost every person was showing some decline, but the amount of decline in many was negligible, and the loss of intelligence they experienced was so slow that it carried most people well into the eighties before it became a problem. For many people, the problems never became severe until shortly before death.

Now here is the important point: This <u>crystallized</u> intelligence can be studied by Bible scholars because it turns out to be approximately what Solomon called wisdom. And according to Proverbs, wisdom is found <u>most often</u> in the seasoned, older person. Solomon, himself, the wisest man who ever lived, continually

---

[1] Schaie, K.W. (Ed.) <u>Longitudinal Studies in Adult Psychological Development</u>. Guilford Press. New York.

admonishes us with the first words of many verses being "my son." Proverbs 8:1 says, "My son, hear the instructions of thy father, and forsake not the law of thy mother." In other words, in age there is wisdom. "Get wisdom, get understanding: forget it not . . . ." (Proverbs 4:5). "Get wisdom: and with all thy getting get understanding." (Proverbs 4:7).

Accomplishing Mental Tasks Quickly

Is there a real difference in the abilities of young and older persons to do a complex task (like solving a difficult arithmetic problem) quickly? Yes, there is. Older persons have about as much ability to solve complex problems as do younger folk; but, in general, advancing age causes older folk to need a little more time.

Researchers have dealt with so-called "speeded tasks" using young and older subjects. The results confirm what most of us would expect. Increasing age causes the brain to function somewhat slower as a rule. I don't think we ought to get uptight about this—it isn't usually important.

But, of course, it could be important. Slowing down is not the same as declining. So, as a general rule, folk do slow down in their thinking. They can get the job done, but it takes a little longer. So what?

Well, I see no need for us to get defensive about this. Actually though, it really might make a difference in the kind of job you do. Some jobs which require speed may be better off in hands of younger folk, and that's a good reason sometimes to move over and let a younger person do it. We don't have to take a back seat. We are all subject to change. The thing I will not allow you to do is to sell yourself short. If the change in your intellectual skills is a result of your age, I'm in favor of your realizing the fact. But if the change in your intellectual skills is brought about because you are getting upset and depressed about it, I don't like it! If you are listening to a lot of wrong information plus listening to your own voice telling you you've had it, you are going to get me upset.

I've already passed seventy, and I must tell you that I know I've slowed down a little in my ability to handle real complex problems. But that's only a little. For the most part, I only let the younger folk do what I didn't really care much about doing anyway. I have changed some in my intellectual skills, and I'm sure I'll change some more. But I wouldn't change places with anyone. Would you?

I hope you like being the one you are—the <u>very</u> one you are. You've got to do that if you live according to God's plan. He does give us choices. The most important choice we have is to choose the attitude we have about things just the way they are. That's important!

Can You Maintain Your Intelligence by Improving Physical Fitness?

Sure you can! If you want to maintain your physical fitness what do you do? Well, several things, of course. You exercise and eat right among other things. And keeping physically fit helps your I.Q. remain relatively stable.

A study performed in 1980 (Elsayed, Ishmail, and Young)[2] even went so far as to show that the same people do better on some I.Q. tests after doing physical exercises than they do before doing the exercises. I guess the exercises at the very least send more blood to the brain. Any toning up of the body is going to have a helpful effect on the brain, you can be sure; although you must remember moderation is a watchword in all things. Inactive, sedentary people show the most

---

[2] Elsayed M., Ishmail A.H., and Young R.S. "Intellectual Differences of Adult Men Related to Age and Physical Fitness Before and After an Exercise Program." <u>Journal of Gerontology</u>. Vol. 35, 1980. 383-387.

decline in intelligence, all other things being equal (Schaie and Parham)[3].

But there is another kind of exercise—mental exercise. Sure physically healthy people maintain not only physical health but intelligence as well better than unhealthy people. After all, the human body is one unified system and not just a bunch of separate parts. It should be obvious that the condition of your heart, lungs, muscles, and blood chemistry affects your brain power. On the other hand, though, there is behavior we can call mental exercise as opposed to physical. Reading books, taking classes, solving puzzles, and math problems are all mental exercises as are word games, conversations with smart people, watching informative television shows, and listening to your minister[4]. There are thousands of mental exercises. Will these exercises keep your intellectual juices going? Absolutely!!

Researchers have shown that mental activity helps performance of an intellectual nature. The more of these intellectual exercises you do, the longer you will maintain your brain power. Did you know there is a strong link between the amount of education you have and how well you maintain your intelligence? It's been proven time and time again. I guess it's just another example of the old saying, "Use it or lose it."

[3] Schaie, K.W. and Parham, A. "Stability of Adult Personality Traits; Fact or Fable?" Journal of Personality and Social Psychology. 34, pp. 146-158.

[4] Gribben et al. "Complexity of Life Styles and Maintenance of Intellectual Abilities." Journal of Social Issues. 36 (2) pp. 47-61.

Chapter 12

HOW IS YOUR MEMORY ?

Remember the days of old, consider the years of many generations . . . (Deuteronomy 32:7)

The most upsetting of all the tales you hear about getting old is that your memory just fades away as you get older. Well, it's true, but probably not like you have been led to think. I wouldn't kid you—your body does decline with age. But it's often not something to get uptight about. To hear some people tell it, it happens dramatically to everyone without fail. If that's so, there must be at least a <u>few</u> exceptions. I myself am one. How about you?

Myths and wild tales are seldom recognized for what they are. Why? Well, mostly it's because there is just enough truth in the stories to keep them going. Some people do have poorer memories as they grow older. The really sad part is that so many of us, hearing that we are supposed to become forgetful, really do become forgetful. Are you letting other people decide for you that you are losing your memory? I hope not.

Remembering Is Hard Work

Having a good active memory means that you must put forth an effort—sometimes a big effort. Really, it has always been that way. Even for the youngsters, remembering is work, but they know intuitively how important it is and automatically work at it. Many folk get lazy about remembering things like names and telephone numbers. They don't make any effort to remember, and they say, "Well, after all, I'm getting older you know. I'm not supposed to have a good memory." And sure enough, they don't. They don't depend on remembering things to make them a living like the young businessman does, so they don't care enough to work at it.

Well, okay, I want you to go to work and remember this: You and only you can determine whether or not you have a good or a poor memory. If you want to take the easy way out and get people to feel sorry for you, if you want to give up your job, or if you want to put things off on your children that you could do better yourself, you can do that. Most people, including your children, are not going to contradict you when you tell them your memory is failing. They have been snowed by the same tales that you have been snowed by.

Sometimes, the young folk are glad your memory is fading. Children and others are not all alike, but they somehow may be glad to hear that you are fading out. If you fade out; they can fade in. Some of them would like nothing better than to take over for you.

You do not have to go along with the idea that failing memory is a burden all older people have to bear. The fact is, you can improve your memory at almost any age. People, no matter what their age, who believe this can develop better memories than they had when they were twenty. Try this: Make up your mind you are going to remember all the important telephone numbers you have to deal with. Then, work at it. The first three numbers of any phone number are always easy. Usually, you can associate these first three numbers with parts of the city where the people you know live. In our town the 776 numbers are in a pretty high-class part of town, while the 799 numbers are in a small adjoining town, plus a large rural area. Find out about the geographic coverage of your exchange numbers (the first three). Then, concentrate on the last four numbers. Try to see them in your mind. Repeat them over and over again. See if any of the last four numbers are the same as the first three. Then, say the entire number aloud a time or two. Last, after you have committed a lot of numbers to memory, go the phone and call these numbers. Call all of them you want to remember, even if you have to make up excuses for calling people.

Let's Be Honest

You are likely to be saying, "Doesn't that man know about Alzheimer's Disease?" The answer is, "You bet I do." That's a really scary thing for older folk. Remember, I'm over seventy, and I know what I'm saying is true. I have friends who have had strokes, Alzheimer's, or a half dozen or so really frightening conditions.

These diseases are all frighteningly real, but the worst of it is that a lot of uninvolved elderly folk are panicking. "Could this be happening to me?" they ask. And then they start looking for the signs that it is happening. Well, why not go with the percentages. Less than five percent of people die from so-called catastrophic diseases. So maybe all this hype about Alzheimer's is probably something you should practice forgetting instead of reminding yourself to remember.

A friend of mine over sixty-five did a strange thing the other day. She unplugged her iron and put it in her refrigerator. After she realized what she had done, she really panicked. She really was in terror that she had the beginning signs of Alzheimer's. We talked about it. I asked her to recall something really embarrassing she had done in earlier years. She came up with something she had done as a freshman in college. The building where classes were held had three stories, and her English class was on the third floor. The floor plans for each floor were pretty much alike. She was delayed getting back from lunch, rushed up to the second floor; and, being a little late, with head down she slipped in and sat down in what she thought was her assigned seat. Five minutes later, she realized she was listening to a chemistry lecture. She sat paralyzed for the hour and slipped out unnoticed and unchallenged.

The point of this story is clear. You can do some really silly things when you are 65, but they are often a poor match for what you did when you were 18. But the myth is out to get us, and the media blitz on Alzheimer's doesn't help either. Added to that, some of your friends and loved ones have had strokes and are being placed in nursing homes with problems that everyone calls Alzheimer's whether that diagnosis is correct or not. In fact, Alzheimer's disease has become a catch-all term that physicians, children, and people who love you but are too busy to deal with you use to put you on ice. Pitiful, but true!

What A Brain We Have

Let's face it—the workings of the human neurological system are truly unbelievable, existing as they do only because the Creator is greater than the creature. How is it even remotely possible for something to happen to you when you are five years old, and you remember it sixty-five years later as if it had happened yesterday? Well, it happens because the Lord God created man and woman as superior creatures and when he had done it He "saw everything that He had made, and, behold it was very good."

The Human Body: A Created Miracle

The human body has become the pattern for our age of technology. The invention of the camera would have been impossible if the inventor had had no knowledge of the human eye. It is now said of computers that they are really miniature human brains. The power of the computer to store and then recover information at the touch of a button is possible only because the human brain conceived the computer in the first place, and in the second place built the computer after the model of the human brain. While being extremely useful, time saving, and work saving, the computer is, of course, far inferior to the brain that conceived it and arranged that it be fashioned out of silicon and plastic.

The Human Brain: Super Miracle

The Bible speaks of the heart as the seat of righteousness, and in a general way as the seat of the emotions; in some senses, perhaps, as the seat of motivation and of wisdom. Thus, the scripture has little to say about the brain as an instrument of thinking or of remembering. God inspired the writers to communicate what could be understood by them and their contemporaries. Yes, that applies to us in the twentieth century. In the mind of God there is and there was a total and complete understanding of the functioning of the human brain and of the physical human heart. God understands memory far better than all the intelligent researchers, and he is even now releasing His own understanding through the work of modern researchers.

God and modern researchers know that memory is possible because of the intricate and unbelievable structure He created on the seventh day, the human brain. We know with reasonable certainty that the physical structure of the organs created for memory is the brain, because medical researchers and surgeons know that when certain brain centers are destroyed, memory is wiped out. The brain is our memory bank where everything we ever knew is stored, to be retrieved at our command.

The human brain is made up of over ten billion cells. Cells are grouped together in the brain to form lobes and other structures and each lobe is given specific tasks to do. One lobe is responsible for seeing, another for hearing, and still another for tasting and smelling. Other parts of the brain are memory banks where everything you have ever experienced is stored. Brain surgeons can stimulate certain parts of your brain when you are in surgery, right there on the operating table, and you will sing the songs your mother used to sing to you at bedtime. All of your experiences are stored in that marvelous organ, your brain. Some of them you can get out (retrieve) very easily; others you can't remember at all.

How Memories Get Into Your Brain

Memories get into your brain through your own efforts. You remember telephone numbers because you make an effort to learn them. Learning something can be done very deliberately or very casually. If you learn something only casually, the impact (encoding) on your brain cells is not very strong and that means you will have trouble remembering (retrieving) a casually stored piece of information. Thus, you remember easily those things you learned really well. You can't remember very well what you didn't learn well.

Helping Memory Along

Learning something like a telephone number really well is likely to occur if you think you are going to need that number. You remember your children's telephone numbers because you learn them well with the added incentive of knowing you are going to need them. More than that, you likely use the numbers quite often. Even if you don't call your children very often, you probably mentally repeat those numbers several times a day because you really want to remember them. A dozen times a day you think, "Maybe I ought to call Susie," and whether you do call her or not, you rehearse the number to be sure you remember it, just in case. You surely have rehearsed your physician's number, the number of an ambulance service, or your police department's number. Certainly, 911!

What I am getting at is that your memory depends less on your age than it does on your quality of learning. People lay it off on age, but it isn't age per se. It is just that as you get older, you get a little indifferent or lazy in learning things really well, and you don't rehearse them. Older people, who realize this, make up their minds to learn things well and then to rehearse things they think they may need to remember. So it isn't age that is the problem; it is your motivation that is at fault—at least most of the time that's the way it is.

Well, you may be saying, "Who wants or needs to do all that much remembering, anyway?" That's okay with me. I just don't want you to get down on yourself saying you can't remember because you are getting too old. That's a cop out. You can cop out if you want to. That is your privilege. But, don't give up a job claiming a failing memory when that isn't truly the case. You may have a dozen good reasons for quitting work, and that's fine. Maybe you want to smell the roses instead of working. Again, fine; just keep it straight why you are doing what you're doing. Your age is probably not a factor in your ability to remember. Of course, if you have a stroke or brain disease that condition will be a factor; but then, even very young people have strokes or brain disease.

Short and Long-term Memory

I am sure you've heard people say that they can remember things that happened a long time ago better than things that happened yesterday or last week. Well, that's understandable. You see those things that happened long ago were probably very important things to you and were impacted on your brain very forcefully. Added to that, you have probably been remembering those things over and over, telling stories about your childhood years, laughing with brothers and sisters about the crazy things you used to do "when we were kids." You see, you have been rehearsing those things all along the way; and we all know that in the rehearsing sometimes people sort of "spice up" the events of childhood. The things you did last week probably weren't that exciting in the first place and in the second place, you probably haven't rehearsed them by telling others about them.

These are interesting and important points. Here are some more. When people get really old (and it varies from one person to another), they may have a loss of short-term memory. Now short-term memory, as the psychologists and brain specialists use that term, is not for remembering what happened yesterday or last week. Rather, short-term memory of this sort is really short, say thirty seconds. Somehow, very old persons can't store memories fast, and things can't be remembered unless they are first stored.

Does Your Memory Determine What You Do?

The answer to the above question is yes! This is why some very old people shouldn't drive. When they are entering the street from their driveways and the cars are bearing down in both directions, they have problems. They look to the right and see cars coming; they look to the left and see a delivery truck coming. They are desperately trying to get out into the stream of traffic. They don't have time to store the information about the delivery truck, because they know they've got to look back to the right in a hurry to see if all those other cars have passed and no one else is coming. They see the way clear on the right and pull out right into the path of the delivery truck. Did their short-term memory of the delivery truck fail them? Well, whether or not that's the whole story, they get clobbered. Probably what happened was that the information about the delivery truck never was stored in the brain. So if it wasn't stored, how could they remember it?

Well, it doesn't make too much difference does it? At some point the learning-storing process gets slowed down; we know that. Maybe it starts slowing down a little at a time long before it becomes important. But we do have to face it; sooner or later our bodies are going to decline. And sooner or later elderly people need to consider their activity levels along with reality factors such as eyesight and memory.

Let's Face It

There will come a time when your memory will not be as good as it was twenty years ago or as it is now. True, you can prolong serious decline by working at it. But sooner or later you are likely going to decide the reward is not worth the struggle. Well, so be it. Maybe the happiest days of your life will come after that. Man and woman were made by God, and someday we shall be with Him. Then, whatever we might have lost will be restored.

Chapter 13

LOVE OF FAMILY AND AGING

I will arise and go to my Father . . .. (Luke 15:23)

The prodigal son learned early in life about the sanctity of the family. The writer and physician, Luke, teaches us through example in this story just how valuable our relationship to the Heavenly Father is. We are the prodigal sons, really! It should be obvious that the Christian home and the ties of love that bind within the family become more important as we age.

The Origin of Family

Family bonds originated because of the love God had for His own Son and for His family of which we are a part. Earthly family bonds of love have been severely strained for most of us in our modern world. Many families do remain strongly bonded, it is true. But the rule seems to be that the calls of vocation., of seeking personal identities, of finding one's own place in the sun, and of climbing the ladder of affluence—all these and other factors as well are causing people to place less value on family ties as they grow through young adult and child-rearing years.

As we age, we may continue this separation and separateness. However, most of us feel the need to return to the closeness which only family members can feel for each other. For most of us, our yearnings reach most strongly upward and downward within the direct family lineage to sons, daughters, grandchildren, fathers, and mothers, more so than to sisters and brothers. That is only natural. But the strongest bond of all is between mates.

The increase in life expectancy has had dramatic impact on how families relate. The many years now experienced by people who live on average to seventy-six bring peculiar stresses between parents and children especially. Sadly, it is almost as if parents are living too long, therewith creating stresses that otherwise would not arise. However, changes in culture and society have had dramatic impacts on family life, too. Rising divorce rates, teenage pregnancies, and drug addiction are stark testimonies of that!

The Extended Family and the Nuclear Family

There was a time when persons of several generations lived under the same roof. This was called the extended family. Elderly people were kept at home, were deeply cherished, and found a rich identity in sharing both love and work. Elderly people, during the time of the extended family, were more revered than they are now.

The nuclear family is often cited as the modern family form. In the nuclear family, there is no place for the elderly. Husband, wife, and a child or two make up the nuclear family. The fact that both spouses work leaves no one to take care of either the young or the elderly. Although it is still true that a majority of widows live with their daughters and that a majority of the elderly continue to sustain themselves in their own homes, there is an increasing need for institutional care of elderly as well as day care for children.

The present elderly are living in a variety of family relationship patterns, but our purpose here is not to discuss these at length. Rather, we shall be content here to discuss problem areas quite common for most of us as we grow older.

Family Relationships Can Be Boon or Curse to the Elderly

We who are 50-plus sometimes are being parents to our own parents while having at least children and grandchildren of our own. We are known as the "sandwich" generation because we are sandwiched in between several generations who need us so desperately that withdrawal would be impossible, even if we desired to rest on our laurels.

Stresses Mount with Increasing Life Expectancy

We 50-plus people have a full generational layer above us—our mothers and fathers—and possibly even another generational layer represented by our grandparents. Most of us have at least two generational layers below us.

There was a time not very long ago when being fifty gave people the right and privilege of resting on their laurels and allowing younger folk to shoulder most of the stress. But with several generational layers of responsibility below us and at least one generational layer above, few of us are relieved of stress. As a matter of fact, our stress levels are likely to rise. This is especially true because we have the frail elderly still with us. It is easy to understand why we are so severely stressed.

Stresses Mount With Increasing Life Expectancy

Many in the Deep South use age fifty as a changing point and call the children together to announce a changing of the guard. One young man, an advisee of mine at Baylor, came in one day in tears. He wanted to go on to graduate school. His family was wealthy, having large farm holdings in western Texas and virtually owned a small west Texas town. The family owned the bank, the grocery store, the hardware store—almost everything.

But Dad had turned fifty, and not only did he tell my advisee that he was turning the family businesses over to him but he also told him that it was the young man's duty to come home and take charge. The young man was in love with a lovely girl at Baylor, actually hated farm community life, and knew he would lose the girl if he should go back to manage the family holdings. The outcome? He did leave the family. Happily, there was an older sister who was delighted to take over. But the young man's anguish was terrible.

In a way, I guess we have to admire this wealthy farmer who refused the stresses and wanted to follow family tradition in turning everything over to his son. Most of us, whose heritages do not embrace this notion, have gone with the flow which demands continued involvement. Thus, our stress levels are likely to rise. This is especially true because, even at seventy, some of us still have frail elderly people in their nineties who require much from us.

On the other hand, the 50-plus person is much closer to the heartbreak problems of children and emerging grandchildren than to his own mother and father. And if his mother and father have become infirm, he has parents to deal with and sometimes grandparents as well. Again, whether or not we are fifty or seventy, we have become parents to at least two generations, one above and one or two below .

It Can't Get Much Worse Than This

Consider Sally who at seventy-five is a healthy and hearty widow. Her husband died five years ago. Sally's parents have both passed on to be with the Lord, but she is the chief caretaker of husband Carl's ninety-two year old mother, who lived with Sally and Carl until Carl died. Her mother-in-law's current residence in a nursing home was accepted by her quite ungraciously. She never really understood why Sally couldn't care for her at home. She is filled with rancor for having been abandoned.

Sally makes at least three visits per week to see Carl's mother, taking her special things to eat and seeing that she is not too lonely. Sally feels these are the "Christian" things to do. She is right.

Carl and Sally had three children of their own, while they created a good life of considerable affluence. Carl left Sally "well-fixed" with ample savings and a nice income. It is too bad that Sally couldn't keep her financial status a secret from at least two of her children.

Daughter Carole, now fifty, has a recently married daughter finishing the university and a son in medical school. Sally's son James Edward has a good dental practice but is an alcoholic. Carole and James Edward live in the same city as does Sally. Maxwell, the third child, has moved to another city, has gained independence, and is a joy to Sally when she sees him—likely only once a year. There are seven grandchildren in all, two of them married. No great grandchildren yet.

Financial Pressures of the Young-Old

We shall use Sally's situation to make a number of points. All three children obtained good educations before Carl passed away. One would think all would be financially independent. Not true for either Carole or James Edward.

James Edward, although ostensibly a successful professional, has been in financial hot water since his marriage. James Edward's wife spends more on clothes in a month than Sally allows herself in a year. Both of James Edward's sons drive expensive sports cars, and James Edward is no penny pincher either. Sally has rescued James Edward from one financial debacle after another. Sally has had to bail him out of jail for DWI twice in the last month. His dear wife simply calls Sally and tells her that her son is in jail again.

Daughter Carole has a near derelict husband and three very expensive children. She has tapped Sally's till time and time again. The latest drain on family fortune (controlled by Sally, yet out of control) was the granddaughter's very extravagant wedding, the expense of which by some weird implication fell upon Sally's dwindling pocketbook. Sally is watching her funds drain away since she has to pay the nursing home costs for Carl's mother, maintain her own household, and pick up the financial slack for James Edward and Carole. Unless she calls a halt to the pattern now in place, she will be shouldering responsibility (financial and other) for a new set of great grandchildren. Sally feels guilty that she is quietly glad Maxwell had the good judgment to move away to another city.

Sally is getting worried! No amount of money could weather the tides now engulfing her finances. Will there be anything left for Sally—even enough for institutional care in a few more years? We all have been privy to these scenarios wherein the money-giver winds up with nothing and has to live on Medicaid. What can and what should Sally do? That's a tough question, and I'm not sure any of us could do any better than she is doing. Ideally and logically, she should call the family together and explain why she must withdraw financial support. But nine chances out of ten, if she does that, she'll be sorry.

It may be that Sally must turn to the Lord with her problems. Her solace and guidance should be placed in God's hands. Only He can see her through this morass.

Inheritances in a Time of Aging

Actually, all three of Sally's children are on the verge of becoming senior citizens. Yet, two of them are still dependent on Sally for bail outs. Is this right? If not, then who is wrong? Yes, you are right—Sally is wrong and has been all these years.

But these things are difficult to handle. What elderly person can say "no" to any adult child who has fallen on bad times regardless of whose fault it is? Not many of us can do it! Much of the time, the adult children, by implication, are issuing veiled commands to us implying that we owe them. Some will actually say, "Mother and Daddy, why don't you just go ahead and give me my inheritance now while I can still enjoy it."

The reasonable facts are that adult children should forget about or at least never count on an inheritance, and it is up to us to see that they understand this. The elderly may cherish the idea of leaving the children a nest egg. But the years have become too many and medical costs have become too high to uphold the idea of expected inheritances.

We have worked for fifty years or more, have provided well for education and vocational opportunities, and have stood by our adult children emotionally. Logically, we should not indulge our children to live better than we do just because we are foolish enough to want this for them and they are foolish enough to accept.

Again, we are the sandwiched generation. Some of us may have been fortunate enough to have received substantial inheritances ourselves. But in this last ten years of the twentieth century, the likelihood is that the elderly have worked hard and adult children have been spoiled. We did the spoiling; maybe we deserve what we are getting.

Some Adult Children Are Gems

It is immensely refreshing to see adult children dedicated to elderly fathers and mothers. And, or course, some adult children deserve many stars in their heavenly crowns because of their unselfish dedication to Mom, Dad, and other elderly family members. Those of us who visit or work at nursing homes these days see this dedication quite often. But in the main, it is sadly not that way at all.

Are adult children right when they place themselves and their young families first? Yes, of course, they are. That is the Christian thing to do. Are they right to withdraw moral, financial, and emotional support from aging mothers and fathers? No, of course they are not right. That is not the Christian thing to do. But aren't our adult children members of the sandwiched generation, too? Certainly they are. Some are sandwiched between us, their fathers and mothers, and their own children and grandchildren. So what can we comfortably and confidently say about all this?

A Return to Love

A large part of the overriding problem is that we have yielded ourselves to stress and worry and have lost sight of the love principle. It is easy to do.

Consider Paula and Dan. They are in their early fifties. Their three children are in their early to mid-thirties. There are five teenage grandchildren with the oldest entering the university this fall. The other four are lined up and expecting exciting university experiences. They are looking fondly to their glorious futures.

But there is not that much money. Paula and Dan received bounteous educations and helping hands from their parents. Do they owe the same to their children? Of course they feel they do!

Three parents remain. Paula's father, who was quite well-to-do, passed on a few years ago leaving the estate in the hands of Paula's mother who at sixty-nine is a fierce guardian of a sizable family estate. But Paula's mother isn't the giving type. Paula feels deeply that Mother should see the problems facing her and Dan. Even a few hundred dollars would get them off the hot seat. Sure, she and Dan have a fine home and three cars, but nothing is really paid for. Dan's business interests demand an affluent lifestyle.

Worse! Dan's parents never had much of this world's goods. They are fine people but didn't think at all in terms of creating wealth. And now, they are both sick, both being in their late seventies. They still live in the family home which is deteriorating just as their health and finances are deteriorating. Both should be in a nursing home, but they refuse to sell the old house, get on Medicaid, and enter a home. It would be such a relief if they only would.

Dan is driving himself to the breaking point, in spite of his bad heart, to see that his parents are well-cared for; and Paula, a sincere people-oriented Christian, does all she can, fixes food constantly, and takes both of Dan's elderly parents to the doctor. Paula has taken it on herself with her grandchildren's help to get these dear people to their church at least twice during the week.

Oh, how Paula worries about Dan's heart problem. He had a triple bypass a year ago and the doctor recommends rest and no stress. "Oh, Mother," she thinks fervently as she sees those university costs coming, "can't you kill the fatted calf right now and give us a little help?"

Can We Avoid These Dilemmas?

Can you see from these examples of Sally and of Paula what a mess longer life expectancy has thrown so many of us into? Let us accept for the moment that everyone's hearts of love are "in the right places." Does it matter that much? Yes, it does.

The bills may be piling up while seemingly senile young-old and old-old hold on to molded money. People 50-plus struggle with health and finances. People of 70-plus grieve over what seems to them neglect and health problems. Indeed, gross neglect is evident in the nursing homes, and we all shudder when the media appropriately focuses on the horrible neglect of the frail elderly.

The crass commercialism of some of the grasping manipulators of human misery appalls us, and we know many of the practices used in bilking the elderly are everything but Christian. We often recognize some of our own reactions and behaviors stemming from our excesses of stress as unChristian, too.

143

But there must be enough love to go around. Somehow, we must calm ourselves and know that God is not dead. He may be testing us severely, and we must indeed pray for guidance and for succorance. But He never leaves or forsakes us, even though our lives are fraught with vexations.

The Line of First Defense

There is not a single one of us who has been able to escape the vexations of growing old ourselves and the pressures of having aging people, both younger and older than we ourselves, around us. Family bonds are undoubtedly strained to breaking points, and we can always find fault with the seeming selfishness of people who we think could make a difference if they only cared enough.

We should be more guardians of our own Christian virtue than detractors of those who at least seem not to measure up, those who seem neglectful, grasping, and selfish. God will judge. We cannot help making judgments ourselves; but then, our judgments may be bad because we walk poorly in our own shoes and not at all well in the shoes of others. Each has his own vexations, and each with God's help must shoulder his own load.

Foresight Is Better than Hindsight

Those of us who are 50-plus or even 70-plus may have waited too late for maximal revision of our ways of seeing and doing things. To gain the more perfect insights would require that we should have begun deliberations for our own successful aging while we were very young indeed. That is not very logical. Young people typically cannot face growing old and cannot easily be enticed into thinking so far ahead.

But no matter where we find ourselves along the corridors of our time span on this planet, there are still insights we can develop and actions we can take. True, every case is a law unto itself. The pressures and stresses endured by people of all descriptions are so variable as to make intelligent comment very hazardous. Still, at the risk of being too general, let me offer the following:

On Family Love, Loyalty, and Unity

The teachings of Christ as well as teachings arising from Jewish tradition emphasize filial love, obligation, and unity. The constant references in the Bible to the family of God, to human brotherhood in Christ, to the sanctity of marriage, and to the importance of parent-child bondings, make us know that family members are different from associations among persons of no blood relationship.

The Christian is called upon especially to honor fathers and mothers. Wives and husbands, although having no common bloodlines, are urged to give each to the other the highest honor and esteem—forsaking all others.

On Family Finance

The best part of wisdom for us who are facing the last few decades or even years of life is that husbands and wives stay together. Death will eventually take both, most often the husband first. But so long as it is possible, financial affairs of the spouses should be handled by the spouses and then by the remaining spouse so long as that is feasible. Finances belonging to spouses can be shared with others, but it is best that a measure of candid non-disclosure should surround financial affairs of spouses so long as one of them is capable of money management.

Children and other loved ones may, under joint consent of spouses, receive succorance from family finances. However, as a general rule, dispersal of family finances to those deemed to need these monies should be in the form of loans. This principle does not hold when spouses wish to and are able to make free-will gifts to children or others.

Loans made to family members should be proffered as such, but spouses should by common consent never make a loan they could not afford to consider a gift. Family members, even with due consideration to filial love principles, are often notorious non-payers of loans taken from other family members.

Children As Custodial Agents

Spouses should depend on reputable professionals for financial advisement including investments. There usually comes a time when children must be made privy to all financial affairs of the spouses. When this occurs, all children should be jointly involved even though one may be given a stronger leadership role than the others.

On Inheritances

Thoughts, discussions, and actions concerning inheritances after death or dispersal of so-called inheritances before death of one or both spouses is such a personal matter that the author intrudes only with some general warnings and basic principles:

1. Spouses must be aware that the state of the economy, the possibility of catastrophic illnesses, future needs of the spouses, and unpredictable events including the length of life, makes it impossible to tell how much money is enough for self-sustenance. Except in cases of disabled, mentally retarded, or other types of continuously dependent children, it seems wise

not to divide inheritances before the death of both spouses. To do so might well create adult children who do not muster their own best efforts and resources.

2. The best and most meaningful gift a parent can give a child is self-confidence. Self-confidence does not come from dependency. However, in these days, young adults training to be professionals may need financial help a number of years after they reach age eighteen. Somehow, parents who can afford it must continue support in the measure necessary to insure the maximization of children's potentials.

3. Inheritances should be thought of as gifts of love, not as obligations.

4. When one spouse dies, the remaining one should divide the other spouse's portion of wealth with the children only if there is sure to be a surplus beyond his/her possible needs.

5. So long as both spouses are active and alert, each should will all properties and wealth to the other until disability arrives with arrangements being made in case of unexpected disability or demise. True, the questions surrounding inheritance taxes must be considered.

On Living Arrangements

Neither spouses nor a single surviving spouse should be pressured into giving up his/her home or other cherished properties in order that he/she may be in line for governmental hand-outs.

The best place for older people is in their homes managing their own affairs. Obviously, this sometimes can become illogical and other arrangements must be made. Since expectations determine attitudes, spouses would do well to choose and expect self-management. Given that necessity alters circumstances, adult children should support their parents' choice to remain as functioning husbands and wives and as self-managing home owners as long as possible.

There are expanding myriads of living arrangements being provided by entrepreneurs for elderly citizens who have money or governmental support. It would serve no good purposes to give an extensive review of this great variety of living arrangements in this book. Please permit me to make three suggestions:

1.   Any and every living arrangement made for the elderly is based on the economic welfare of someone other than the elderly person who pays. If there are exceptions, so be it—this author hasn't found any exceptions.

2.   Regardless of attractive features presented by entrepreneurs, such attractiveness is sure to be volatile. If the food is excellent, it will soon not be so excellent; if the nursing care is adequate, it will wax and wane from tolerable to terrible. There is no free lunch, and lunches you pay for are often not as palatable as they appear.

3.   Adult children (at whatever age) should not depend on constancy of any living arrangement made either by parents, by the adult children themselves, or by any combination of interested parties. Constant vigilance, along with periodic changes, is the only way to insure adequacy of these arrangements.

Chapter 14

RETIREMENT—SHOULD YOU EVER?

Take my yoke upon you, and learn of me; for I am meek and lowly in heart: and ye shall find rest unto your souls. (Matthew 11:29)

Every one of us, who performs a regular work task in order to make a living, is aware of the idea that one day we shall retire from work. For the most part, retirement benefits are built into every job situation in industrial and corporate America, and most of us look fondly forward to the eventuality of not working. On the other hand, there are serious questions about the consistent benefits of retiring just because you can do so. So far as the Lord's work is concerned, you need not ever retire until a very few days before you meet the Lord face to face.

Retirement Planning Makes Sense

Those of us who are fortunate have jobs we basically enjoy. The world of work is so large and so varied that vocational choice is a very important thing; we are always urged to give a lot of thought and preparation time with concomitant educational preparation to the choice of vocation. A prime consideration in choosing a vocation is to acquire a job that one really likes to do.

Of course, liking one's work is a relative thing. Any job entails work, and to a certain degree any work has an onerous quality to it. Jobs, no matter how much we may like them, make demands on us and intrude on our lives, requiring large blocks of our time. So almost without fail, when we choose our vocations, a large part of the consideration must be retirement arrangements and benefits.

Approaching Retirement

We approach retirement usually with eager anticipation, counting off the years and months until we can "hang it up." Then too, we make ambitious and detailed plans concerning what we shall do during retirement years—how we shall spend our time doing just what we have always wanted to do. The normal couple approaches retirement with joy and anticipation. The normal couple or person has built up resources to see him through retirement years.

Approaching Retirement with Elation or with Dread

The excitement of retirement varies greatly with how well we have liked our jobs. It also varies with the type work we do. The person who has spent many years in back-breaking physical labor needs to give his body a break and counts the days until he doesn't have to push his body. The worker whose job entails constant pressure of being pulled at by other people, having to humor customers, and having to deal with confusion constantly, feels he needs to give his "nerves" a break. He needs to get out of the stress.

Professional people most often have to be people pleasers and have to work under varying amounts of stress. Some professions are highly responsible ones where human lives may hang in the balance of professional expertise and judgments. Such work generates a special kind of stress. Some professionals reach forward to retirement because hands or minds have become unsteady, too unsteady to risk other lives to their adequacy.

Retiring from work carries for every one of us an element of getting out from under—out from under physical, emotional, or managerial stresses. We just want to get it over with—or at least we think we do. We yearn for the perpetual weekend.

Getting Into Something New

On the other hand, most of us are just as anxious when we retire to get into something new as we are to be done with the old. We want (or think we want) to garden, to fish, to play golf, or to travel. For most of us, it is a combination of getting away from some things and into some other things.

Obviously, the person who retires successfully must do a lot of planning before retiring. We are all smart enough to know that the play we anticipate could become tiresome just as the work we do becomes tiresome. So we must plan for variety. Many plan well and experience long retirements of blissful activity combined with "just doing nothing."

The Years of Retirement May Be Prolonged

Most of us fail to recognize the extensiveness of the retirement years. Sometimes there are a lot of them. It is usually a mistake to set one's mind on a retirement scenario and to expect that scenario to hold us in euphoric states for the thirty or more remaining years. We often find ourselves needing to retire from our retirements. To the chagrin of many of my friends, they have found retirement to be a bore.

As we are experiencing the added years of our longevity, many of us are seeing that a truly successful retirement consists more of changing jobs than of leaving a job behind. Every person has a right to do what he wishes with his retirement. There are some of my friends who truly can enjoy doing nothing gainful for thirty or more years. Maybe they are the lucky ones, and certainly they are entitled to do "their things." Some travel, some putter, some piddle and some are into physical activity.

There Are At Least Two People Involved in Retirement

One thing that must be considered in retirement, where spouses are jointly involved, is the compatibility of the spouses in their choices of retirement activities. It is a fact that greater strains sometimes descend on marriages during retirement years than ever were felt in the routines of working.

It is a certainty that non-working spouses have as great if not greater adjustments to make to the retirement of the worker than does the worker himself. Let me tell you about two of my friends who retired at sixty-five. I decided to stay with my profession until age seventy, and I eagerly watched my friends, thinking Ruth and I could learn a lot from their experiences. Incidentally, I am afraid that people often cover up some retirement woes. They are supposed to be happy, so they put on happy faces. On the other hand, some are eager to freely express disappointments and miseries of retirement.

Louie and Evelyn Summers approached retirement gleefully. Louie was an executive in a large company. He had over five hundred employees under his direct supervision. Almost all five hundred attended his retirement dinner. Louie was showered with praise for a job well done and was assured with much backslapping that "we'll keep in touch, buddy." The couple bought an attractive bungalow on the lake and started their retirement. I saw Louie a few days ago some two years after the big dinner. As I prepared for my own job exodus, I asked him how retirement was treating him.

"We're having a ball, Les," he said. "We have pretty much a routine. One day we fish, one day a week we play golf, and in between we just do what we want to do. We make short trips to places we enjoy, have favorite eating places and favorite friends. We are very active in church, and we're having a ball."

I believe Louie was telling me just the way it was. "Oh yes, Les," he said, "you remember those five hundred people who said they'd stay in touch? Well, in two years we haven't seen a single one of them. We do have a lot of church friends, and it's great to see you, buddy. Why don't you go on and hang 'em up? Don't worry, it's great!"

While I did believe Louie implicitly, my mind couldn't help but reflect, "Just how long can all this happiness with doing all the little things you always wanted to do last?"

Stewart and Dorothy Jumper presented quite a different story. Stewart had been a corporate attorney and Dorothy a legal secretary. They retired at the same time by common consent although both could have continued a little longer.

"We're miserable," Dorothy volunteered. "Stewart is like a caged tiger and so am I. He's driving me nuts being around the house all the time. He was supposed to plant a big garden. Take a good look at his fine crop of weeds! He played more golf when he was working than he does now and enjoys it a lot less. As for me, I think I am going bananas."

It is quite a let-down for people to find they miss the old job and associates as they look at countless meaningless years that stretch ahead. One wife of a retired golfing buddy told me, "For a lot of years we had teenagers to entertain for three whole months at a time during summer vacations. I felt like I'd go crazy before they got back in school in the fall. I always celebrated that glorious event for weeks. Well, 'you-know-who' is worse than six teenagers all wrapped into one, and it's going to last forever. I'd give anything to get him off my back." Of course, she was half kidding—but only half.

Retirement—A Long-term Goal

Most of us simply cannot envision a thirty-year or even a twenty-year retirement. We typically make retirement plans as if they were going to last only a few years. When we began our marriages, we did so knowing our lives for the ensuing thirty years or so would be lived out in logical patterns. There would be the adaptation phase, the child-bearing stage, the child-rearing stage before formal schooling, the teenage years, college perhaps for all, and then the empty nest stage. We were prepared for a stage-wise, living-out of our years at least up to our fiftieth birthdates.

We don't typically do that *vis à vis* retirement. We are not prone to plan retirement beyond a general conception of "what we are going to do during retirement" either spoken or thought of as if it would be one span of time.

Long-term Retirement Requires Several Stages

As a psychologist dealing with aging persons over a thirty year span, I have observed a number of cases both among my own parents, the parents of friends, and most recently among my own clients. Let me give you two anecdotes:

Alice and Tom Huston retired at sixty-two because Social Security benefits were tailored to encourage retirement at this early age. When Tom retired, so did Alice, both of whom had starry-eyed expectations about traveling and taking life easy. That was twenty-five years ago, and I know what has happened to at least one of these two people. Perhaps, the worst should be related first. Alice, now eighty-five, is in a nursing home with multiple medical problems including a recently-acquired broken hip. In her most lucid moments Alice talks a lot about Tom and the wonderful life they had together. These pleasant memories are a plus for Alice.

In reality, the Huston's marriage lasted for five years after their retirement. Both of them got tired of traveling within a year. Their plans for retirement included nothing but expected good times. At sixty-seven, Tom opened a new decorating business expecting Alice's support and help. Actually, he chose this business because Alice encouraged it since she was quite artistic and Tom had had a career in selling.

The business folded in less than two years, and in that interim the two fell out of love because of squabbles over the business. It was downhill after that. They took bankruptcy on the business, and after the divorce both remarried. Alice married a much older man, and he passed on soon after. I really don't know that much about Tom except that he married a much younger woman.

Jade and Vera Levine planned their retirement carefully. Although it didn't seem to me that they fully understood the longevity principle of retirement, they must have picked up more from our discussions or from their own ingenuities than I thought. They were heavily into a playful retirement. That is not necessarily a bad thing, but few of us can play more than a year or two without loss of vital meaning for our lives.

But Jade and Vera learned quickly that they couldn't play for twenty to thirty years. Two years after retirement, Jade want back to his old job as a consultant (Luckily, he had valuable, almost irreplaceable wisdom in his field.). He stayed on at half-time and three quarters pay for ten years.

Then, Jade and Vera played for another year or so. Vera had taken on a great deal of volunteer work visiting for the church. She was among the young-old; and being full of energy and being people-oriented, her life was full to overflowing. Jade started his private consulting business at seventy-eight. His office is in his home, and he is enjoying his work immensely.

In his recent book, Age Wave, Ken Dychtwald and Joe Flower offer the following statement:

> And since most older people would enjoy a chance to continue working but in a more flexible, less pressured fashion, the key to redefining retirement will lie in a restructuring of the way we work and the ease with which we are allowed to interweave work and nonwork throughout our adult years.[1]

Emerging Patterns of After-Retirement Work

There are some companies even now who are forcing employees toward retirement, while many others are suffering a loss of expertise in having to let valued employees go because of mandatory retirement rules as well as through the loss of employees who decide to retire early. Thus, many companies are eager to accommodate the special needs of retired workers.

Retraining

Many workers are retiring early and voluntarily because they are seeing their effectiveness waning because they do not have the high-tech skills needed for work or for further promotions. With this, many companies including IBM and Ford are engineering retraining into the workplace. With special retraining, many employees are able to continue, and many are able to progress into new and different jobs.

Retraining is not necessarily exclusive to industry. Many individuals are putting their own retraining into force by going back

---

[1]Dychtwald, Ken Ph.D. and Flower, Joe. Age Wave. Jeremy P. Tarcher, Inc, Los Angeles. 1989.

to community colleges and technical schools for further education, usually specifically technical.

For some, the choice is to enter a totally new line of work. Most of us have been happy with our jobs, but have always wanted to try something new. Some of us have worked hard at hobbies throughout our lives, and these hobbies can be expanded into profitable business ventures with retraining and refocusing.

For many people, money-making is not a chief concern of after-retirement ventures. Dychtwald and Flower correctly point out that the sought-after goal in post-retirement should be new experience rather than money per se. At the same time, most of us who take up second careers will feel elevated by the new experiences only if our ventures are successful. And, perhaps unfortunately, making money has become the principal way of keeping score in our society. An aging person does not have to think of the pros and cons of leaving larger inheritances through his sustained efforts at pursuing a second career. There are many excellent ways of disposing of money.

Volunteerism

The world of health and social service would collapse except for volunteer workers. Many elderly people are deeply involved in volunteer work. My wife Ruth refers to herself as a professional volunteer. Hospitals were the recipients of her dedicated work for many years. Nursing homes are now her focus.

Some say volunteers are not properly appreciated. Indeed, institutional professionals sometimes have negative views of volunteers. To some extent, volunteers are seen as replacing professionals.

Never doubt that your volunteer efforts are blessed by God and that you can be fulfilled by your work! Only in the frustrated minds of some unreasonable paid workers is volunteerism sometimes held in disrepute. Please know that your volunteer work is a missionary work highly meaningful to yourself, a good example to others, and a faithful service to a needy world.

Affluent Retirement

Statistics reveal that more than eighty-five percent of America's men and women over sixty-five do not work. This does not necessarily mean that they will never work again.

However, it is true that there are many highly affluent Americans who move from affluent work lives to affluent retirement. It is worth noting that there has been an explosion of retirement communities geared to affluence. Sun City near Phoenix, Arizona is a prototype of these communities. These are age-segregated villages which provide active lifestyles for the elderly while not overlooking the longevity principle of retirement. People who are flocking to these villages are never without full lives and excellent socialization in these communities. Over one million retirees are now residing in such villages in Arizona, Florida, and California. For those who relish and can afford these lifestyles, there are few negatives. Self-esteem need not suffer because of affluence, and there is no dearth of opportunities for affluent retirees to do the Lord's work in countless ways.

Many Retirees Really Need Financial Help

On the other end of the spectrum, it is the rule rather than the exception that retirees need financial enrichment to make Social Security and pensions adequate for their needs. So, for many, to continue working is a boon not only to self-esteem but to being able to afford something a little more than the bare necessities.

Flextime

Some companies depend heavily upon part-time workers among retirees. The nature of some businesses is that they are seasonal and that it is costly to keep a roster of full-time workers on hand as opposed to a large pool of part-time workers.

Flextime allows workers to come either when needed or when they desire. Granted, there is difficulty for management in matching company needs with part-time workers' desires. However, many companies are very willing to allow great leeway to older workers who "write their own tickets" so far as number of hours worked and times when work is done is concerned.

Flexplace

It is certainly true that some business enterprises have always allowed or even required workers to perform at home. The drapery company which has decorated several houses for Ruth and me has always required their employees to work at home. Not only do workers set the place, they set the time of work and the amount of hours worked also.

Beware the Manipulators

It seems necessary to take notice of some employers who solicit part-time work from the aging community and expect to pay a pittance for services, thus taking advantage of some aging persons who must work in order to survive.

But over against this hateful reality, many reputable companies are making attractive situations for worktime and workplace to suit the desires of workers available, especially to their own retired workers.

All Work and No Play

Most of us are well aware of the workaholic personality, of Type A's as opposed to Type B's, and of other forms of compulsive needs to work, work, and work.

The retired person must seek a balance between his needs, his desires, his leisure time, his social life, and his health. What we do with all this is in our hands. Let's maximize our lives! Work hard! Play hard! But be sure you live to see the sunrise! Never give up, but do take time to smell the roses. With Ulysses; a character provided to us by Alfred, Lord Tennyson; let us say:

Come, my friends,
'Tis not too late to seek a newer world.
Push off, and sitting well in order smite
The sounding furrows; for my purpose holds
To sail beyond the sunset, and the baths
Of all the western stars, until I die.
It may be that the gulfs will wash us down;
It may be we shall touch the Happy Isles,
And see the great Achilles, whom we knew.
Though much is taken, much abides; and though
We are not now that strength which in old days
Moved earth and heaven, that which we are, we are—
One equal temper of heroic hearts,
Made weak by time and fate, but strong in will
To strive, to seek, to find, and not to yield. [2]

---

[2]The Norton Anthology of Literature, Vol. II, Revised, M.H. Abrams (ed.) pp. 841-43.